MW01434160

OTTAWA REWIND 2

MORE CURIOS AND MYSTERIES FROM

OTTAWA REWIND 2

MORE CURIOS AND MYSTERIES FROM

ANDREW KING

OTTAWA PRESS AND PUBLISHING

OTTAWA PRESS AND PUBLISHING
ottawapressandpublishing.com

ISBN (pbk.) 978-1-988437-43-9
ISBN (EPUB) 978-1-988437-44-6
ISBN (MOBI) 978-1-988437-45-3

Printed and bound in Canada

Design and composition: Magdalene Carson at New Leaf Publication Design

Front cover illustration after painting by Andrew King
Courtesy Gordon Gibson

Library and Archives Canada Cataloguing in Publication

Title: Ottawa rewind 2 / more curios and mysteries from Andrew King.
Other titles: Ottawa rewind two
Names: King, Andrew (Artist), author.
Identifiers: Canadiana (print) 20200294261 | Canadiana (ebook) 20200294733 | ISBN 9781988437439
(softcover) | ISBN 9781988437446 (EPUB) | ISBN 9781988437453 (Kindle)
Subjects: LCSH: King, Andrew (Artist)—Travel—Ontario—Ottawa. | LCSH: Ottawa (Ont.)—History. | LCSH:
Ottawa (Ont.)—Description and travel.
Classification: LCC FC3096.3 K56 2020 | DDC 971.3/84—dc23

For Maggie the Wonder Dog,
my faithful friend and sidekick for so many years.
Her adventurous and daring spirit will be with me always.

CONTENTS

Introduction *ix*

Acknowledgments *xi*

1 The Springs of Cathartic *1*

2 The Lost Loonie *5*

3 An Apple by Any Other Name *8*

4 When Humpback Whales Swam through Ottawa *11*

5 Beers of Bytown *13*

6 Before There Were Road Signs *18*

7 The Killing of Hostess Chips *23*

8 Ottawa's Forgotten Pandemic Bridge *27*

9 The Story behind that Totem Pole *30*

10 Canada's Air Force One *33*

11 The Legend of *The Wishing Tree* *36*

12 The Ottawa River's Mysterious Solar Wheel *40*

13 Ottawa's Forgotten Mega-Church *46*

14 First Store in the Valley *50*

15 The First Ship on the Great Lakes *54*

16 From Bells Corners to the Stone Corral Shootout *60*

17 Ghost Train to the Airport *68*

18 The Last Zellers *70*

19 Canada's Cursed Candy Kiss *73*

20 What's Up with That Island Behind Parliament Hill? *78*

21 Sir (Sir) John A. *82*

22 The Chateau Laurier and the *Titanic* *85*

23 Can't Find Coke in a Bottle? — Become an MP *89*

24 A Folk Hero and a Sunken Fort *91*

25 The Avro and the Iroquois *97*

26 The Last Stand of New France *102*

27 Hartwell's Silver Lining *109*

28 A Missing Ottawa Sign *113*

29 In Search of the First House *115*

30 Tale of the Guardian *121*

31 The Mystery of the Vanier Bunker *127*

32 Remembering the Green Valley *131*

About the Author *136*

INTRODUCTION

Thank you for reading *Ottawa Rewind 2* and joining me on more history rambles. My sincere appreciation goes out to you, the reader, and everyone at Ottawa Press and Publishing for making the first *Ottawa Rewind* such a success.

I am thrilled to learn we have common interests — learning more about the obscure and curious history that is all around us. Collaborating once again with the talented team at Ottawa Press and Publishing, we are thrilled to bring you another compendium of historical mysteries and curiosities from Ottawa, and for this edition, a few places beyond.

The story of the world's oldest maple tree is one of the stories from a place beyond. But we couldn't resist putting that story in this edition. After reading it, you'll see why.

Like the story of the world's oldest maple tree, I continue to be astounded at the fantastic history tales that are all around us, but rarely get taught in school.

History always evolves. There is always evidence yet to be discovered that can drastically change the accepted framework of history. A theory once thought to be impossible, can suddenly become fact.

The *Ottawa Rewind* project is meant to shine a light on our past, and the stories that have been overlooked by history books or faded from our memories. Please join me once again on these new adventures, exploring the untold and hidden facts of history.

Andrew King
2020

ACKNOWLEDGMENTS

It is with profound appreciation that I thank the readers and fans of *Ottawa Rewind* for making our first book such a success. The overwhelmingly positive response to the book was truly encouraging and it was great to know so many others share my passion for local history. My thanks to all those who braved the Ottawa elements last year in order to attend book signings across the city, and those that made the book a gift to friends and loved ones. It was a distinct pleasure to meet and chat with each and every one of you. Having readers share their own personal stories with me was rewarding, and our conversations were full of fascinating, forgotten history.

I'd like to thank the many bookstores and wonderful staff at each of them. You continue to bring the magic of books to so many during challenging times. All of you contributed greatly to the decision to go ahead with this second book.

I'd like to thank the many institutions and companies that make historical data available for research, both online and in-person. From the Ottawa Public Library, Library and Archives Canada, the City of Ottawa, to Google News Archives, GoogleMaps and GeoOttawa, you have all provided an incredible resource for the curious minded.

This book would not be possible without the wonderful team at Ottawa Press and Publishing. Ron Corbett shares an enthusiastic passion for local storytelling and I'm grateful he believes i*n Ottawa Rewind* and was committed to making this second book a reality. Magdalene Carson of New Leaf Publication Design created a beautiful book that was carefully curated for maximum enjoyment, and her amazing work is reflected here once again.

The year 2020 has been a challenging year for all of us, and I sincerely thank you for choosing to spend both your time and resources on what you are about to read. I hope it offers a chance to escape for a moment and allow you to slip away to simpler times, invoking happy memories, a taste of curiosity and an appreciation for the hidden history that lies around us.

OTTAWA REWIND 2

MORE CURIOS AND MYSTERIES FROM

THE SPRINGS OF CATHARTIC 1

The word cathartic comes from the Greek word "kathairein," meaning "to cleanse, or purge." Catharsis later became a medical term for purging the body of toxins, and soon people started using the word cathartic to mean an emotional release, or spiritual cleansing.

Just a few kilometres east of Ottawa there once was a hamlet called Cathartic. It got its name because of the many bubbling mineral springs in the area, springs that were reputed to have healing and spiritual cleansing powers. The hamlet's name was later changed to Carlsbad Springs. (Sadly, according to Goggle Maps, the memorable place name Cathartic is no longer in use anywhere in the world.)

Drive through the "Springs" today and it is hard to imagine the bustle and frenetic pace that would have been here in the later part of the 19th-century, when people from across North America came to Carlsbad Springs to take a dip in its many creeks and streams.

The healing waters of Cathartic were incredibly famous for a while, and a number of resort hotels, even a CN train station, was built in Carlsbad Springs. Then, just as quickly as they were built, the train station and hotels were demolished, the visitors went away, and the bubbling streams seemed to vanish.

Can any of this wonderful history still be found in Carlsbad Springs? I decided to find out one day, and feeling a bit like Ponce de León, I went in search of Ottawa's forgotten Fountain of Youth.

↑ The village of Cathartic in the 1890s. The Dominion Springs Hotel is in the background.

Spring Is Here

Many of my history rambles start by looking at maps, and that's what happened this time. While looking at an 1879 map, I noticed a small town outside Ottawa called Cathartic. The name would catch anyone's attention, and when I peered more closely I saw Bear Brook creek ran through the hamlet.

I started doing some research and soon learned that Bear Brook creek, off Russell Road, was once part of a First Nation's trail that linked what are today Ottawa and Montreal. The trail became Russell Road when pioneer settlers came to the area in the 1850s.

The natural springs surrounding Bear Brook creek were soon noted by the settlers for their mineral content. The water bubbled up from subterranean aquifers, through ancient bedrock. Before long there was a mill on the creek — Boyd's Mill — and the hamlet surrounding the mill was named Cathartic in 1870.

Shortly afterwards the first hotel opened in the area, built by the Dominion Springs Company, which touted the healing properties of the nearby springs and creeks. By 1892 another hotel, and a train station, had been built in Cathartic and there was a steady stream of visitors from the nation's capital and beyond.

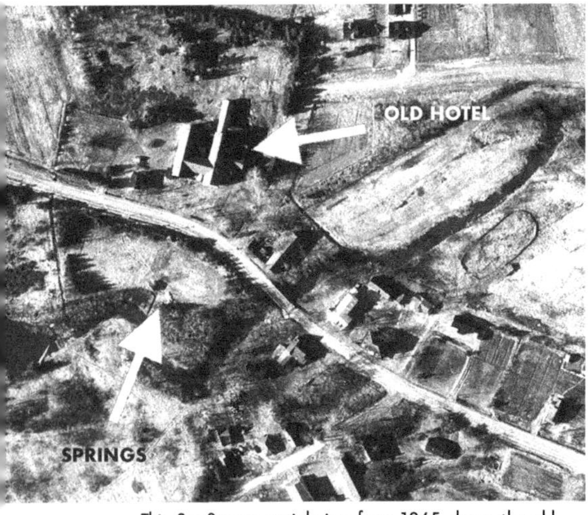

This GeoOttawa aerial view from 1965 shows the old hotel still standing.

Again, it may be hard to believe today, but Ottawa's largest dance hall was once located in Cathartic. Ottawa's first bowling alley opened in Cathartic. And yes, Cathartic was Carlsbad Springs.

By the start of the 20th-century the local mineral water was being bottled and sold throughout North America. In a display of feverish capitalism not normally seen in Ottawa,

Cathartic was even "rebranded" in 1906 and given the name Carlsbad Springs. The name change was openly acknowledged by residents as a marketing ploy to lure European visitors to the area. (Carlsbad is the name of one of the oldest mineral spas in Europe, built in the Czech Republic in the 14th century by the King of Bohemia.)

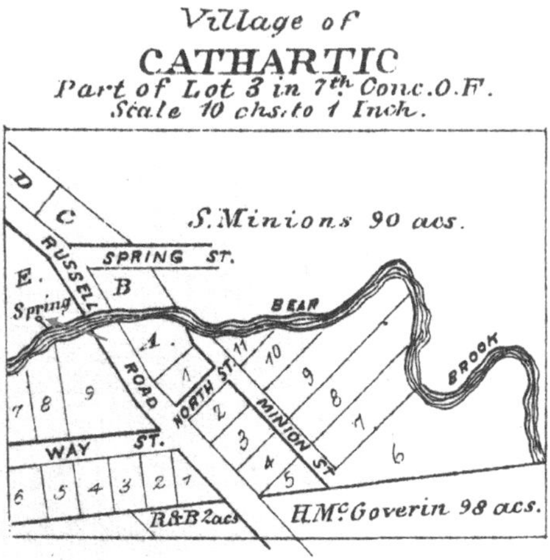

The springs surrounding Bear Creek were also given names based on the properties of the waters from them: Soda, Sulphur, Magic, Lithia, and Gas. Water from those springs was bottled and sold under those names.

It would all disappear during the Great Depression — the resorts, the train station, the bathhouses and bottling plants, the dance hall — none would be around by the end of the 1930s.

But surely the streams are still be there? Right?

My Ponce de León Moment

An old map of Cathartic from 1879 shows a spring next to Bear Brook creek, and another small stream leading from that spring. Comparing that to a modern Google Map of Carlsbad Springs, it reveals that nothing much is there now, and the old road on the 1879 map has been shifted south.

Heading out to Carlsbad Springs and walking along the muddy shoreline of Bear Brook creek

↗ The 1879 map above shows the springs of Cathartic.
→ At right, what is left.

to where the spring was marked on my map, a trickling sound was soon heard. I followed it to a small spring.

The source of the cathartic waters were right there in front of me, still bubbling up from the earth. You could see the almost oily nature of the water, with a film of some chemical on top of the bubbling water.

I managed to find the spot where a promotional photo was taken in the 1890s, but it looks unrecognizable today. A quick survey of the area revealed more old springs and their own particular properties, as mentioned earlier. Some were moss laden. Others were rust coloured.

At one spring I found an old glass bottle that looked like it would have been used for bottling water, back in the hey day of Cathartic. I still find it amazing how often you find historical artefacts like these around Ottawa. All you have to do is spend time rooting around in the woods, and you find them.

And a busted glass bottle may be an appropriate symbol for the little hamlet outside Ottawa that once had a name no other place on earth ever claimed — Cathartic.

An old harness from Cathartic.

A mineral springs bottle.

THE LOST LOONIE 2

Canada's dollar coin was originally designed to look much different than the coin we know today. The first design had to be altered after a mysterious theft in 1986.

Our story begins in 1982. That was the year the Government of Canada first started talking about taking the dollar bill out of circulation. After four years of polling, surveying and focus-grouping, the government announced on March 25, 1986, that a new dollar coin would go into circulation the following year and the dollar bill retired. The government said the move would save taxpayers $200 million over 20 years (the calculation is based on the greater longevity of coins versus paper currency.)

The new coin was made so it matched the dimensions and weight of the American Susan B. Anthony dollar coin, which already worked in many vending machines in Canada. The new coin would have a voyageur image on it that was already being used on the rarely circulated Canadian silver dollar. The new coin would be bronze-plated nickel and it would have 11 angled sides.

The voyageur design and specifications were approved, and the master dies prepared in Ottawa. When the dies were ready they would be sent to Winnipeg, where the dollar coin would be minted and put into circulation.

And than a funny Ottawa-sort-of-thing happened. Someone in the federal government decided — quite unexpectedly — to try and save some money.

They Did What?

A coin die pair, showing both sides of a coin.

The Royal Canadian Mint in Ottawa.

In order to save $43.50 in shipping costs (try to imagine that being a lot of money in 1986) a never-identified official at the Royal Canadian Mint decided to send the master dies not by way of armoured-truck delivery, but by way of a local courier.

The voyageur master dies were packaged and shipped from Ottawa on November 3. Perhaps in an attempt by this unknown official to save a further $43.50, the dies were sent as one shipment. (There is a worldwide convention among currency manufacturers to always send master dies as two packages, so the two sides of a coin are never together in one place, except at a mint.)

Mint officials in Winnipeg waited eleven days before notifying Ottawa that the shipment was, ah, how do we say this — late. Three days later the RCMP were called in — but the shipment never came.

For several weeks the mint kept the disappearance a secret, in hopes the dies would be found somewhere. The news was even withheld

Dollar fiasco third time mint lost moulds

By Greg Weston
Citizen staff writer

The head of the Royal Canadian Mint admitted today that master moulds were twice lost before the disappearance three months ago of the dies for the new one-dollar coin.

Maurice Lafontaine, master and president of the mint, told a Commons committee today that on one occasion a box containing a set of master dies fell out of a delivery truck in between plants in Hull and Ottawa.

The valuable moulds for a complete set of collector coins were later found by a citizen, turned over to police and eventually returned to the mint, a spokesman said. The incident occurred about five years ago.

On another occasion about three years ago, Lafontaine told MPs, a set of dies for transit tokens were lost en route to the southern United States.

"We never did get those ones back," spokesman Murray Church said later.

Lafontaine was called before the Commons committee to explain the loss of the pair of master dies for the dollar coin which vanished in November after the mint tried to ship them from Ottawa to Winnipeg by a regular parcel delivery service.

During his testimony this morning, the mint's master at first said the policy for shipping dies was "not all that clear in writing."

But under questioning from Liberal Don Boudria, Lafontaine later conceded there was no written policy, even after the earlier losses.

Asked if the two previous incidents had brought

(Mint, page A2)

from Finance Minister Monique Vèzina, who was responsible for the mint's operation.

When the RCMP told the Mint the dies were probably stolen, they briefly considered making minor variations to the Voyageur design and proceeding as planned. But it was decided the threat of counterfeiting was too great and a new design was needed.

Artist Robert-Ralph Carmichael.

The loon image we know today is by artist Robert-Ralph Carmichael. His design was originally submitted to the Mint in 1976 — and rejected — during a design competition for Canada's new $100 gold coin. Carmichael died in 2016, but his name lives on in his coin. (Look closely at your next Loonie and you'll see, directly under the loon's beak, between the ripples on the surface of the water, the artist's initials — RRC.)

Already weeks behind schedule, the Mint quickly made new master dies using Carmichael's design and shipped them to Winnipeg (this time the government splurged and paid for an armoured truck.)

The Loonie (and that is the coin's official name. The Mint registered the word as a trademark in 2006) was launched on June 30, 1987. Forty million dollar coins went into circulation that year.

The Loonie is no longer bronze-plated nickel, but bronze-plated steel. This means it is not accepted at many older vending machines. In justifying the switch to steel, the Mint said the new coins produce an electromagnetic signature that is harder to counterfeit, and that by using steel instead of nickel it will provide significant cost savings.

Wait — haven't we heard that somewhere before?

3 AN APPLE BY ANY OTHER NAME

What do Steve Job, a love-struck 18th-century American farmer, and Samuel de Champlain have in common?

This story.

In 1796 John McIntosh — our love-struck farmer — followed his sweetheart from Upper New York State to Canada, where she had moved with her Loyalist parents. Dolly Irwin died before McIntosh found her, but the young man decided to stay in the British colony and seek his fortune.

In 1801 McIntosh married, and in 1811 he purchased land near what is now Dundela, Ontario. While clearing land on his property that same year he discovered some wild apple seedlings.

Apple trees are not native to Canada. They came by way of early French settlers and were in cultivation in the ill-fated Port Royale settlement as early as 1606.

Allan McIntosh with the original McIntosh Red apple tree, circa 1890.

Samuel de Champlain was among the early Port Royale inhabitants, although it is unlikely he had much to do with the apples. There is no record of him being much of a farmer.

The apple trees spread inland (as did Champlain) and McIntosh was so taken by the saplings he found that he transplanted them closer to his home. One of those trees grew to have such good fruit that McIntosh's son, Allan, grafted it and began growing clones.

By 1900 McIntosh apples were the most popular variety of apple in Eastern Canada and the North-Eastern United States. Today it is estimated nearly a quarter of all the world's known varieties of apples (101 of 439) are descended from the tree sapling John McIntosh found south of Ottawa in 1811.

Enter Steve Jobs

That's a lot of apples. And a lot of orchards. In the mid-'70s on an apple orchard in Oregon there was a young picker by the name of Steve Jobs. When Jobs co-founded a computer company a few months after leaving Oregon — and while he was still raving to friends about the positive experiences he had working at "the orchard," — he decided to call the company Apple.

A few years later a young computer designer working for Jobs was nearing completion of the prototype for a low-cost, easy-to-use personal computer. Whether it was to curry favour with a boss who clearly had a thing for apples — or whether it truly was his favourite fruit, as he would later claim — Jef Raskin named his prototype MacIntosh.

Steve Jobs and "Mac" inventor Jef Raskin.

Raskin (who died in 2005) was a smart man in many ways. Fearing a possible lawsuit over the name McIntosh (the apples are trademarked) he added a letter and changed the name of his prototype to MacIntosh.

Was Raskin being overly cautious? Probably not. Steve Jobs had been warned not to use Apple as the name for his company, in case Apple Records — the label founded by the Beatles — sued for trademark infringement.

In 1978 that's exactly what happened. (The case was settled out of court in 1981.)

So what's in a name? Well, as it turns out, quite a lot.

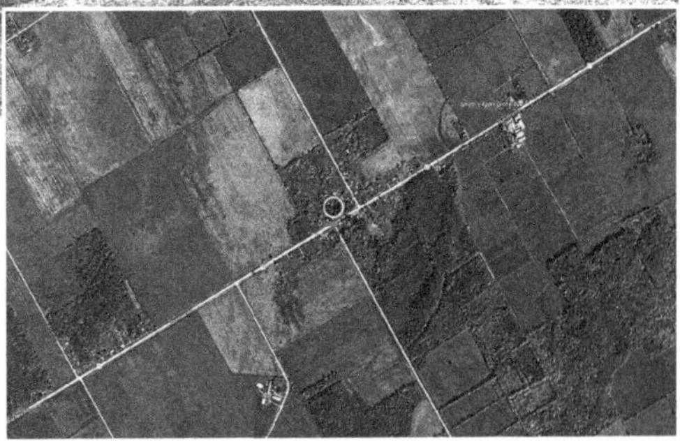

A, historic plaque marks the spot of the world's first McIntosh tree, also shown on Goggle Maps in the hamlet of Dundela, Ontario.

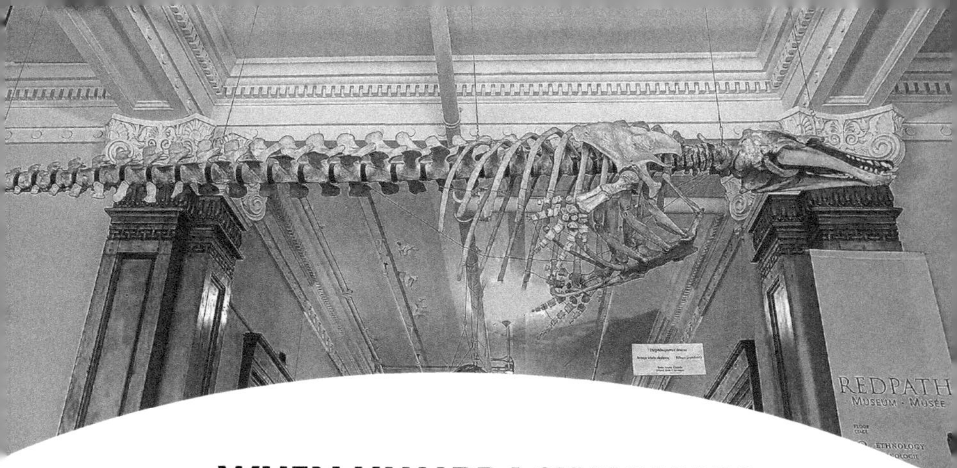

WHEN HUMPBACK WHALES SWAM THROUGH OTTAWA

4

When you're stuck in Ottawa traffic your mind can drift as you stare with glazed eyes at the hundreds of cars slowly moving ahead of you. The snail beside you in the ditch is making better progress.

On one such occasion I began to imagine a time when the nation's capital was under a vast ocean. It was a daydream, yes, but not a dream. Twelve-thousand-years ago melting glaciers created a murky sea that covered our region in about 500 feet of saltwater, from Ottawa all the way to the Atlantic Ocean. Today, that long-ago ocean is called the Champlain Sea.

Imagining this ancient sea that once existed above our heads, I also imagined the many sea creatures that would have swam above us long ago, and how their remains must be buried in the soil around us. A quick bit of research back home showed me that such a find did occur once. A creature of the ancient Champlain Sea was discovered in 1874 south of Ottawa.

And that creature turned out to be a humpback whale.

The story is told in a report published by Princeton

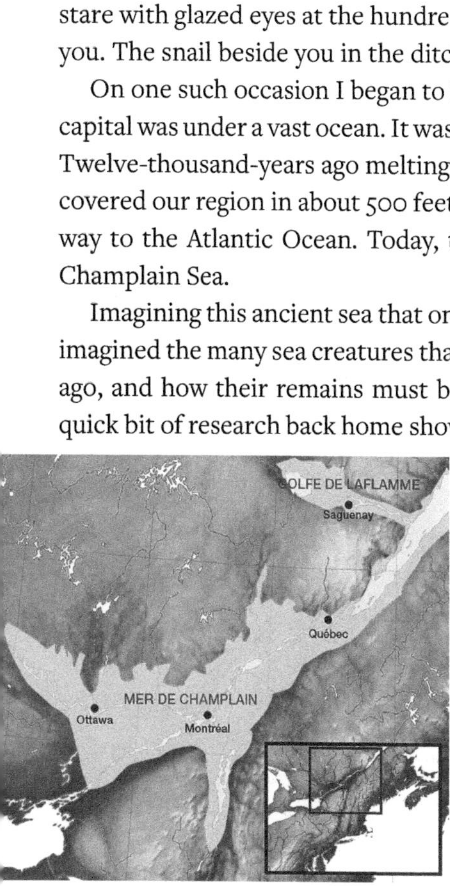

↑ Skeleton of a whale from the Champlain Sea, near Ottawa, displayed at the Redpath Museum in Montreal..

Showing the size of the humpback whale found in Ottawa.

University in 1883.The report tells of the discovery of the remains of a humpback whale near Smiths Falls in 1874. It happened when a Canadian Pacific Railway line was being built through the town.

The report — it was an inventory report, primarily, of the Peter Redpath Museum in Montreal — explained that the bones were found in a gravel pit three miles north of Smith's Falls at a depth of 30 feet beneath the surface. Two vertebrae and a fragment of another, along with a portion of a rib and other fragments were found.

The bones were donated to the Redpath Museum, which still houses them today. In addition to this humpback whale, the remains of at least *seven* other whales have been unearthed in the Ottawa Region. In 1948, at a sandpit near Uplands Airport, the remains of two beluga whales were found. It seems the sandy bottom of the Champlain Sea is where a number of whales were laid to rest 12,000 years ago, with many more likely waiting to be found.

Sandy soil, like the sand hills around the airport, are an indication you may be looking at what was once the floor of the Champlain Sea. Look toward the sky and imagine an ocean surface five hundred feet above you. It's a fun daydream. Try it. (So fortunate we are to have those sandy hills near the airport. The intersection of Hunt Club Road and Riverside Drive may be the worst place in the city for rush-hour traffic.)

Sand hills are where you'll find whales.

BEERS OF BYTOWN 5

Here's a fun fact you may not know. When Ottawa was called Bytown (1826-1855) we had more taverns and drinking establishments than *any* other kind of business. For most of those years it wasn't even close.

Having trouble believing that? Let's go further. For many of those same years (building the Rideau Canal, the years right after) there were more taverns and bars in Ottawa than every other business *combined.*

Indeed, so notorious was the reputation of Ottawa back then, when the city was chosen as capital of the new country of Canada, most of the public service in Lower Canada (Quebec) refused to come.

The Town That Fun Forgot? You should have been here in the day. (Or maybe not –the notorious Irish street gang the Shiners ran the city for many of those years.)

Ottawa's first tavern predates construction of the Rideau Canal (Firth's Tavern was featured in *Ottawa Rewind*) by nearly a decade, but where did all that beer come from? Was it all shipped in? Seems unlikely. So where was Ottawa's first brewery?

That would make a good history quest.

Does Anyone Know a Good Brewery?

My research started, luckily enough, by finding a wonderful account of those early drinking years. *Ottawa Food: A Hungry Capital,* was published in 2014 by Don Chow and Jennifer Lim. They say it is difficult to be definitive on the

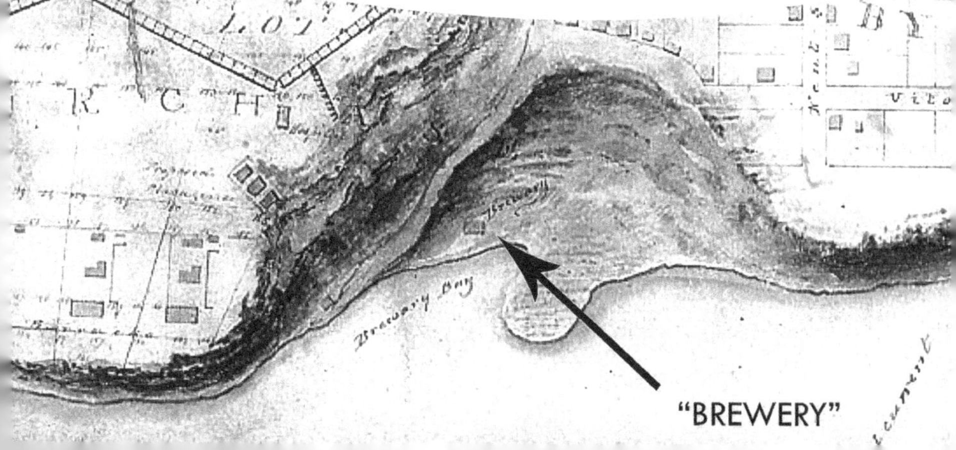

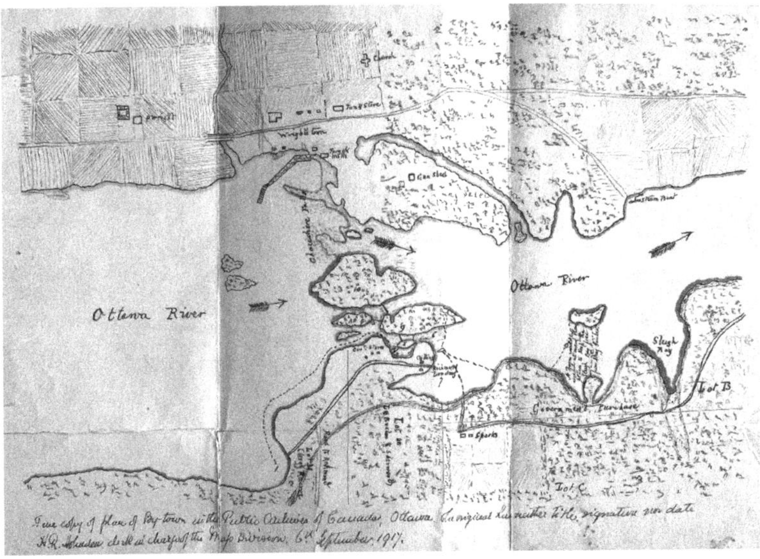

This 1825 map shows Ottawa the year before construction started on the Rideau Canal.

point but believe Ottawa's first "official" brewery (not a vat in the woods) was "The Victoria Brewery." That brewery operated from 1829 to 1899 at the corner of Rochester Street and Wellington Street.

If you're running that address through your head I'll wait a minute. That's right — it no longer exists.

The Victoria Brewery was in the heart of Lebreton Flats, the community razed by the federal government in the early '60s as a part of an urban renewal project that never happened. The brewery was founded by John Rochester, and it reportedly produced a double stout and an India Pale Ale.

But *was* this Ottawa's first brewery? If the start date for The Victoria Brewery is accurate — 1829 — it means the Rideau Canal had already been under construction for *three* years. Had no one thought to brew a vat of beer in a city that had more taverns than stores and streets milling with thousands of itinerant labourers looking for something to do?

Seems unlikely. My search continued

↻ This 1831 map shows a brewery, just to the west of Parliament Hill.

A Second Contender

A great piece on *Bytown.net* says that in 1819 Ralph Smith from King's County, Ireland, built a house near Richmond Landing. An excerpt from *An Irishman in Canada* published in 1877 by Nicholas Flood Davin says that a man with the same name built the first house on the south shore of the Ottawa River, across from Philemon Wright's settlement (the second house was built by Nicholas Sparks.)

According to Davin, after building his house "near Richmond landing" in 1819, Smith started operating "a brewery and a ferryboat," the same year. (The ferry service was to transport people and goods across the river to Wrightville, now Gatineau.)

If Smith did build a brewery in 1819, as Davin claims, that would predate The Victoria Brewery by a decade. And would make it, probably, Ottawa's first brewery. (Perhaps not coincidentally Firth's tavern opened the same year.)

Sounds good. Now — how to prove it?

Don't Tell Me It's Under Water

Old maps have always fascinated me. The information they contain, — the place-names, the geographical features — they are all links to a time that was never photographed. I can sit down and pour over old maps for hours. One such map, held by Library and Archives Canada, is labelled MIKAN 4135481 Bytown 1831.

The map was drawn to show the topography of the riverfront of what is now Parliament Hill — back then Barrack's Hill — and it clearly labels a body of water on the south shore, just

Readers' Remarks

Yet another terrific glimpse into Ottawa's past. As with all your posts, you provide a great deal of insight not normally available to the casual citizen/historian. — *Stephen*

I made the same discovery in May 2013 on the map of Burrows (in French.) I like your work with the Burrows map and the satellite photo. — *Henri*

It can be tricky lining up old waterfronts. Yes, partly due to flooding as you mention, but also because in this case the pathway below the Hill is all on landfill. Early photos can be found that show the Hill dropping straight down to the water. Yes, there was a low, sloping area between the Hill and where the Supreme Court is now, which is where the brewery may have been located, though that also got filled to create the current parking lot. — *Mark*

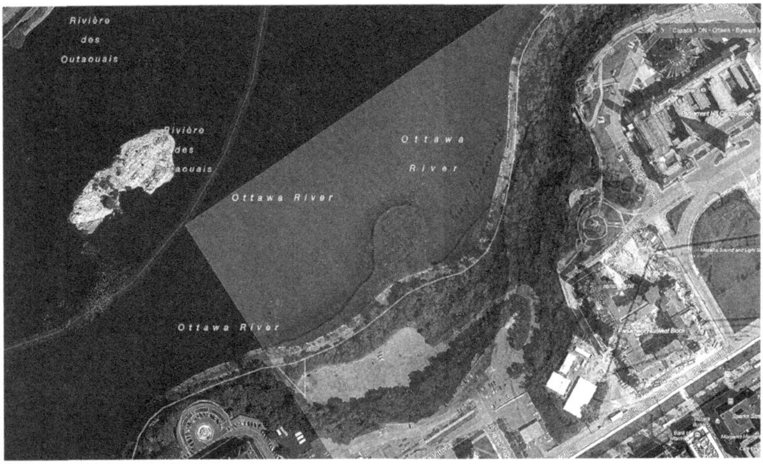

By placing the 1831 map over a Goggle map of the area, we can see where the remains of Ottawa's first brewery may be hiding.

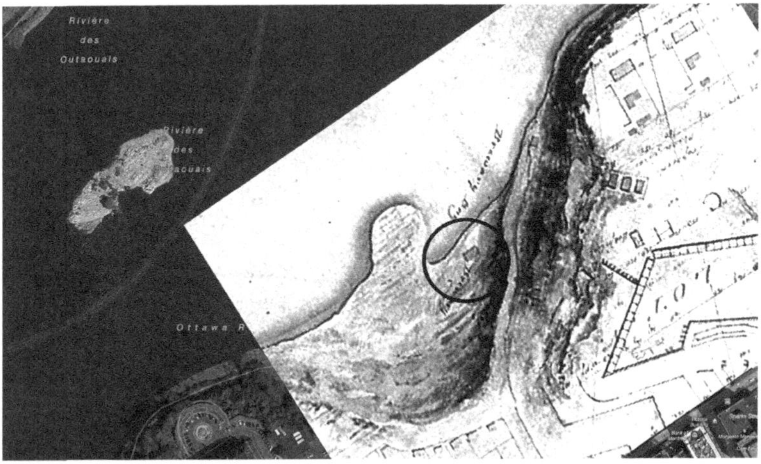

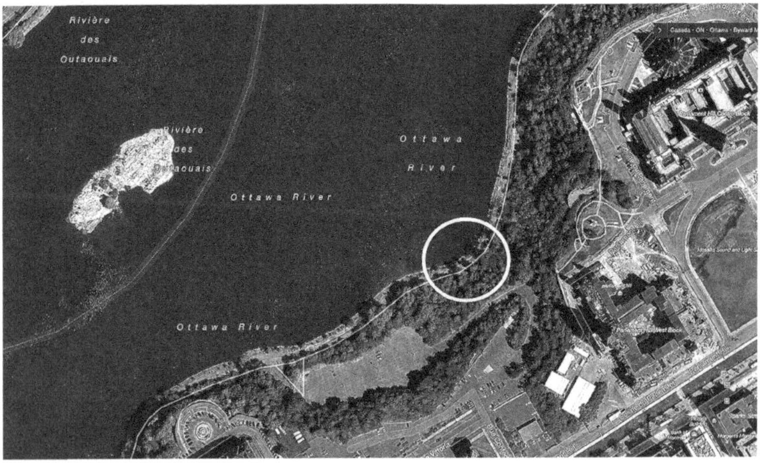

west of the Hill, as Brewery Bay. When I look closer, I see a small building there, labelled "brewery."

Bingo. This is likely Smith's south-shore brewery.

But there are other things I notice, when I overlay a GoggleMap of the area. The shoreline has changed. The original shoreline — along with the brewery — is probably underwater today, the result of rising water levels after building the Carillon Dam.

But — that isn't certain. When I look again at the overlays I see that Smith's brewery may have been saved a watery demise. It seems to be just far enough inside Brewery Bay to have escaped the flooding that made the peninsula disappear.

It is possible there are some remains of the first brewery in the wooded area off the bike path that runs along the shoreline, as shown in the accompanying images.

There are also some stone blocks visible on Google Streeview that look like they may be from an old building. It is also possible my initial fears — it's all under water — are true and this is just wishful thinking on my part.

This is a mystery that — temporarily — is stumping me. If anyone has information on Smith's brewery, The Victoria Brewery, or any other brewery that may be in the running for title of Ottawa's First Brewery, I'd love to hear from you.

Brewery Bay, looking east down the Ottawa River.

6 BEFORE THERE WERE ROAD SIGNS

A hike through an undisturbed forest is something of a treat. One can clamber over rocks and plants never traversed by others, escaping the crowds and busy roads of the city. These days, with cell phone apps and GPS to guide our way, it is not easy to get lost in the woods. However, I've learned that trekkers long ago had their own version of a GPS: a strangely bent tree.

The Mystery of the Crooked Tree

Before a network of highways and roads guided us across this country and before the arrival of Europeans in North America, Indigenous people used a network of marked trails and paths to travel safely across the continent.

Back then, there were no signposts, rest stops or tourist information centres to point travellers in the right direction. Instead, trail blazers built trail-marker

A bent tree in the woods near Opinicon Lake, seen in the distance (↑) and close-up (←). The tree is pointing toward the lake.

trees: bent trees that pointed passersby in the right direction. Once saplings bent with rawhide or vines, they are now mysteriously shaped, full-sized trees.

When a friend told me about trail-marker trees, I was skeptical. Nature can behave strangely, giving us oddities that seem to defy any natural explanation. I thought bent trees were just natural anomalies — until I came across one.

There, high on a rocky ridge, was the definite shape of a bent tree. Its presence caught my eye, much as it would have attracted the attention of a forest traveller many years ago. Upon closer inspection, it became clear that this tree could very well be a trail marker.

How Bent Trees Were Made

To make these markers, Indigenous people usually used saplings of oak, maple, elm or other hardwoods that were easy to bend. They then used animal skin or wild vines to tie them to stakes or rocks. In a 2013 interview with Indian Country Today Media Network, Don Wells — co-author of *Mystery of the Trees* — explained, "These trees would be bent as saplings, when they were about ¾-inch in size,

An illustration of mine, showing how bent-tree markers would have been made.

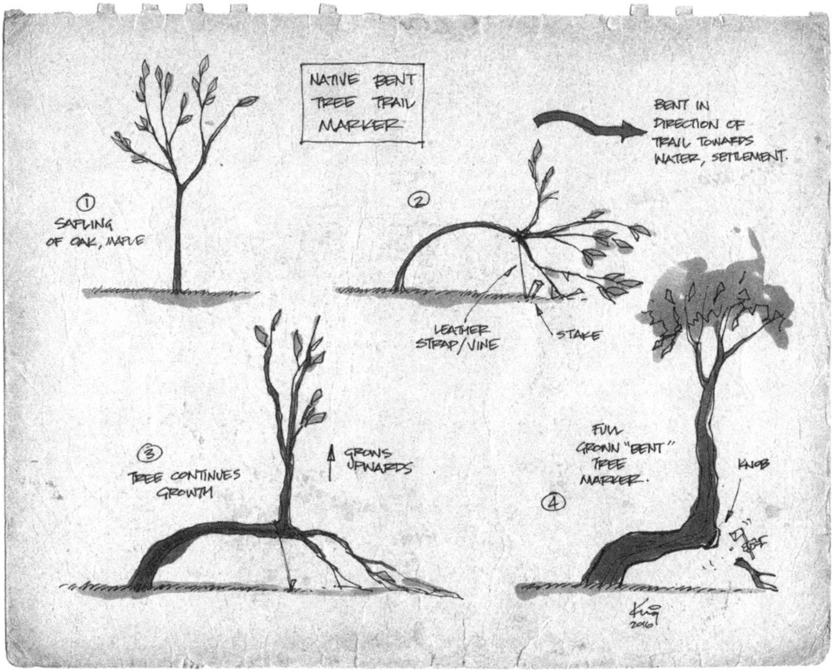

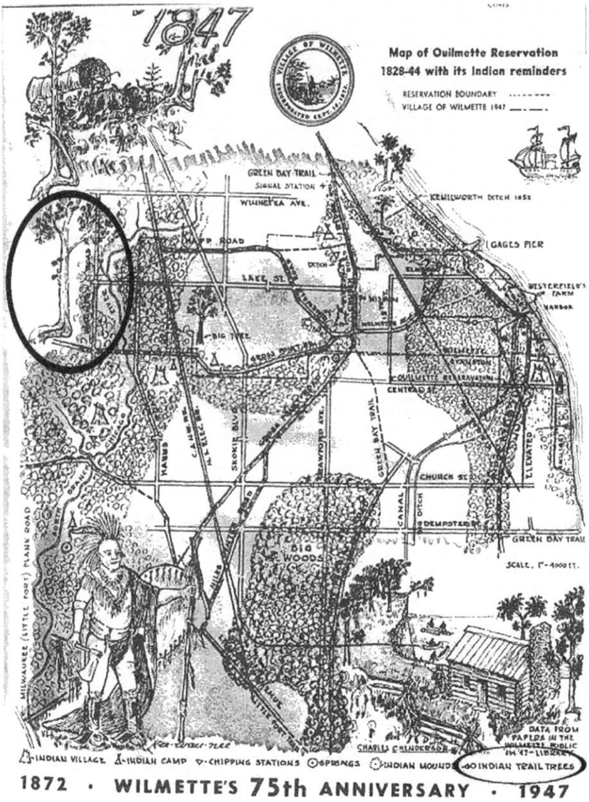

A map of bent-tree markers near Wilmette, Illinois.

and tied down. They would be left that way for a year and lock into that position."

As a bent sapling grew, its side branch would grow upwards, and later form the main trunk of the tree. The bend of the tree would be a few feet off the ground so the horizontal trunk could still be seen in the deep snow of winter. Sometimes, a hollow would made in the bend, so people could leave behind message sticks or other parcels.

The Bent Tree System

The direction in which the tree was bent would indicate the proper direction to the traveller. These marker trees were often created on high ground for visibility and would usually point out the best route to a waterway, a settlement or a lake.

Dennis Downes, president and founder of the Great Lakes Trail Marker Tree Society, explains further on the society's website. "Some of these trees would have brought them to fresh water springs, the preferred source of water used by the Native Americans and settlers alike. Other Trail Marker Trees would have guided them to areas with exposed stone and copper deposits needed for their adornments, hunting implements, and everyday tools. Yet others would lead them to the areas where they could gather medicinal plants as well as plants used to make their dyes and paints. The Trail Marker Trees would have taken them to ceremonial sites and occasionally the burial sites of their ancestors. Also, in relation to the rivers, these trees would indicate areas of portage and safe crossing (fords)."

The first record of trail-marker trees appears in a document called *Map of Ouilmette Reservation with its Indian Reminders dated 1828–1844*. This map includes actual drawings and locations of existing trail-marker trees.

At least as far back as 1940, articles have documented the existence of these trees in the Great Lakes region. In 1965, archaeologist Robert E. Ritzenthaler wrote an article in the *Wisconsin Archeologist* that claimed any trees 200 years of age or younger would have to have been made by European pioneers copying the practice of Indigenous people. European settlers also used ancient Indigenous routes to build rudimentary carriage roads, which became the paved roads we use today.

Discovering the Bent Tree

On a trip to Opinicon Lake, I travelled down a winding, narrow road between Highway 15 and the Rideau Canal's Davis Lock, previously used to transport rock used in the canal's construction from a quarry in Elgin. High on a cliff, I noticed an unusual tree that matched the description of the marker trees my friend had told me about. I grabbed some gear and hiked through the forest to inspect the tree. Sure enough, it was a strange bent tree, pointing toward Opinicon Lake and the connection between two lakes.

Further inspection revealed another bent tree on nearby high ground. It seemed to be consistent with the old bent tree practice: on high ground, bent toward a place of interest, along a very old road that was most likely once a trail.

Since pioneers are thought to have followed the Indigenous practice of bending trees to mark a path, the one I found may have been made early settlers during construction of the Rideau Canal. Or perhaps Indigenous people marked the trail to point the way to the waterfalls of Opinicon Lake (whose name comes from a native word for "potato").

The Rideau River was once an important route used by Indigenous people to travel between Kingston and Ottawa, so finding a trail marker tree along it is not unusual. The tree also had a hollowed-out area in the bend. It was fascinating to see one up close. I will not dismiss the possibility that it is of natural origin, but the evidence and research seem to prove otherwise.

Are There More Out There?

Many of these unique bent trees have been lost to road construction, development or logging. However, some may remain as living pieces of history. Who knows how many more are out there waiting to be found, lost markers to the past, silently awaiting their next visitor?

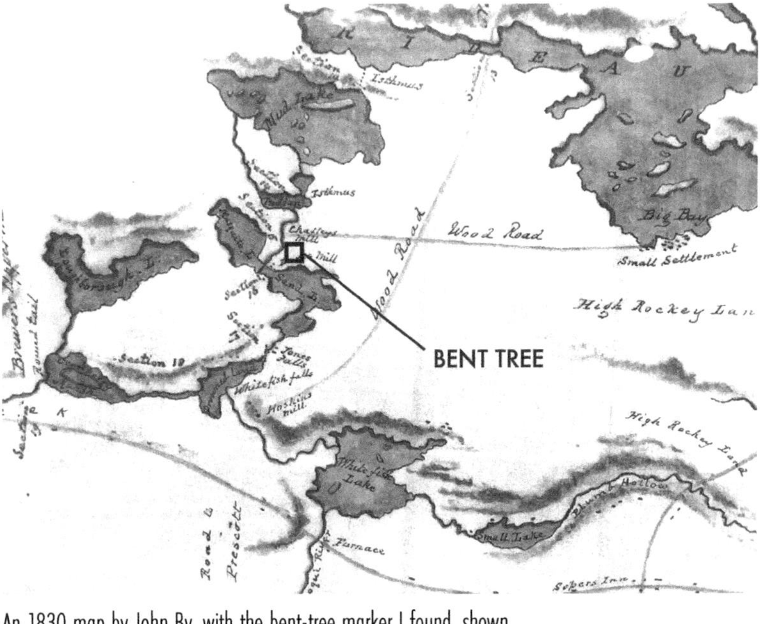

An 1830 map by John By, with the bent-tree marker I found, shown.

THE KILLING OF HOSTESS CHIPS 7

Childhood memories are an oasis for the mind in today's challenging world. Recalling nostalgic events or products brings us a brief moment of joy reflecting on those more innocent times. For me, BMX bike rides to the Becker's convenience store after collecting bottles from the ditch is one of those happy recollections, as a $2.00 bottle-deposit refund was like winning the lottery. That bottle money was quickly put right back into the Becker's cash register when I bought Wacky Packs, Dinosaur Eggs, Sour Chews and, of course, Hostess potato chips.

The 1980s gave us such great movies, music and junk food. Washing down some fresh foil-bagged Hostess chips with Jolt Cola was an integral part of our teenage lives and, for many, Hostess was THE GREATEST potato chip in Canada.

As our carefree childhood days slipped away, so did our Munchies. In what would be a sly corporate takedown, Canada's beloved Hostess chips were killed by a well-known American corporation: Pepsi.

It Started in Kitchener

The epic Canadian story of Hostess potato chips stretches back to 1935, when Edward Snyder started making potato chips on his mother's kitchen stove in Breslau, Ontario, near Kitchener. One Saturday, he took a small supply to the Kitchener market and was sold out by mid-morning. The potatoes were peeled and salted by hand. He wanted Snyder's potato chips to be of the highest quality. He created foil bags for the chips to retain their flavour and crispness.

Public demand for Snyder's potato chips led Snyder to build a factory on land he purchased that adjoined the Snyder farm. His entrepreneurial spirit and outstanding marketing ability led to his chips being sold in Toronto and across southern Ontario. However, it wouldn't be until 1955 that his chips went big. That's when Snyder sold his chip company to E.W. Vanstone, who expanded it greatly before selling it to General Foods four years later.

Hostess was the new brand, and the chips soon garnered a solid reputation for quality. They were still packaged in foil bags to maintain freshness, and the bags were colour coded by flavour: blue for

Munchie hats and rock-star stickers — Hostess in its heyday.

regular, yellow for salt and vinegar, red for HOT BBQ. These colours were such an effective marketing tool that other brands continue to use them to this day.

Hostess became the #1 potato chip in Canada and fought off U.S. corporations that soon started entering the Canadian chip market. The genius of its marketing once again made waves when Hostess introduced "The Munchies" in 1981.

These three cartoon characters represented the hunger one gets for salty snacks. Widely successful, the Munchies became the brand image for Hostess and were placed on all their chip bags except the bags for Hickory Sticks — those had a wood-grain motif on their packaging.

Hostess was so popular that the company gave away goodies inside chip bags, including rock music stickers, film tie-ins, and Munchie Merchandise prizes. It was the top potato chip brand in Canada and the choice of almost every Canadian kid who bought chips in the 1980s.

American companies were irked that their brands could not compete with the formidable Hostess brand, leading to a plot to eliminate it: a Munchie Murder.

Chip on Their Shoulder

The 1980s were the Golden Age of many things, including snack foods, and corn-based snacks were rising in popularity. Fritos, Cheetos and Doritos were all taking the stage. Hostess didn't have any corn-based snacks and decided to enter the market by partnering with Frito-Lay, which was owned by Pepsi.

In 1987, Hostess and Frito-Lay joined forces to introduce a corn-based chip snack called Hostess Taquitos, and the companies merged in 1988. The Pepsi-owned Frito-Lay now started bringing its own brands — including Ruffles, Cheetos and Doritos — into the Canadian market. In 1992, Pepsi bought out the rest of General Foods' share of Hostess. This would spell the eventual death of the beloved Canadian Hostess brand.

Hostess Taquitos are now Zesty Doritos.

Hockey icon Mark Messier helped Hostess rebrand as Lay's.

Munchie Murder

Pepsi replaced Taquitos with its own brand, changing the name to Zesty Doritos. Yes, your Zesty Doritos are actually Hostess Taquitos.

With the introduction of other Pepsi-owned chip brands, such as Ruffles and upscale chips such as Miss Vickie's (another formerly Canadian chip company, which Frito-Lay bought in 1993), the Hostess brand was effectively destroyed by the very company that purchased it.

Pepsi changed the name of Hostess to Lay's in 1996, using hockey players as spokespersons to rebrand the image of this new chip.

The Munchies were killed off, Hostess chips were quashed, and Pepsi now only keeps the Hostess name on Hickory Sticks.

Now, more than ever, I think we need to revisit the things that make us happy, and bring them back by any nostalgic means possible. If that means that the American corporate Pepsi machine reintroduces the once #1 Canadian brand Hostess potato chips for an upcoming anniversary, then let it be so. Because, in the end, when you've got the munchies, nothing else will do.

OTTAWA'S FORGOTTEN PANDEMIC BRIDGE

8

Like any city, Ottawa is no stranger to quickly spreading viruses. At one point in our history, unfortunate ill souls were housed on an island in the Rideau River, and a hidden and rusting iron-truss bridge that once carried those virus victims still remains.

The year was 1893 and the smallpox virus was sweeping through the nation's capital. The City of Ottawa wanted to build an isolated hospital to keep those infected away from the general population. City council chose Porter's Island, an eight-acre, low-lying property in the Rideau River, as the quarantine station.

An isolation hospital was hastily constructed on the island. To access the island, an iron-truss bridge was built for $5,000 in 1894.

A quarantine camp on Porter's Island, circa 1910.

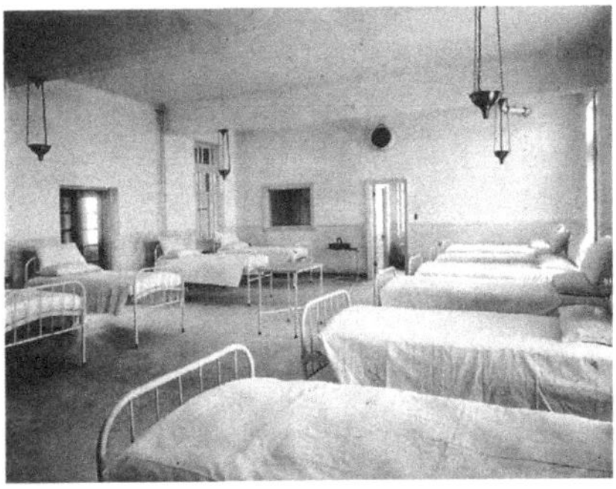

↑ The Sanitary Hospital built on the island in 1912.
← The women's ward.

Those diagnosed with the virus were taken to the island across this bridge, which is still in place today, although closed to the public.

After the smallpox epidemic, Porter's Island became a garbage dump. The abandoned and rat-infested hospital buildings were demolished in 1904, but another smallpox epidemic hit the city and yet another hospital was erected in 1910. This time, it was in the form of tents.

This quarantine camp on the island was short lived. In 1913, the City hired architect Francis Sullivan, who had been the only Canadian student of Frank Lloyd Wright, the famous American architect. Sullivan's design for a new isolation hospital on the island was one of his first commissions in the city. He would go on to design many notable buildings around Ottawa, including the Horticulture Building

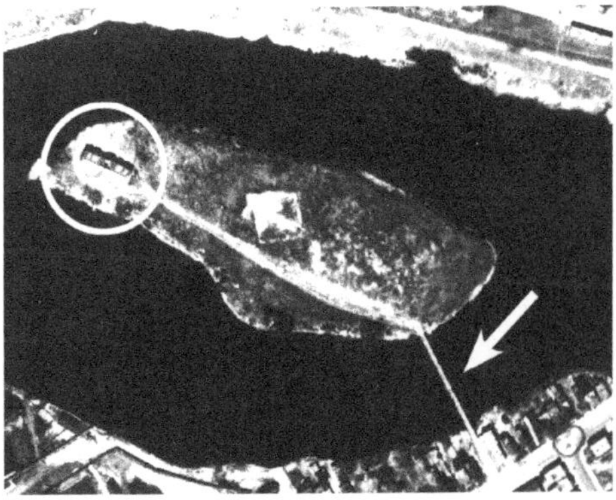

This 1965 aerial photo shows the hospital still standing.

at Lansdowne Park and grand residences in Sandy Hill, Rockcliffe Park and other central neighbourhoods.

The handsomely designed brick isolation hospital reflected the latest contruction techniques, and it remained on the island until it was demolished in 1967.

In the late 1960s, retirement residences were built on the island. However, the 1894 isolation island bridge is still there — off St. Patrick Street, just west of the point where St. Patrick crosses the Rideau River. Closed off, and overgrown in summer, this little-recognized iron bridge is a reminder of our city's pandemic past.

These aerial photos show the demolition of the old hospital (↙)and construction of the current retirement home (↓ ↘). The 1894 bridge to "pandemic island" can be seen in each photo.

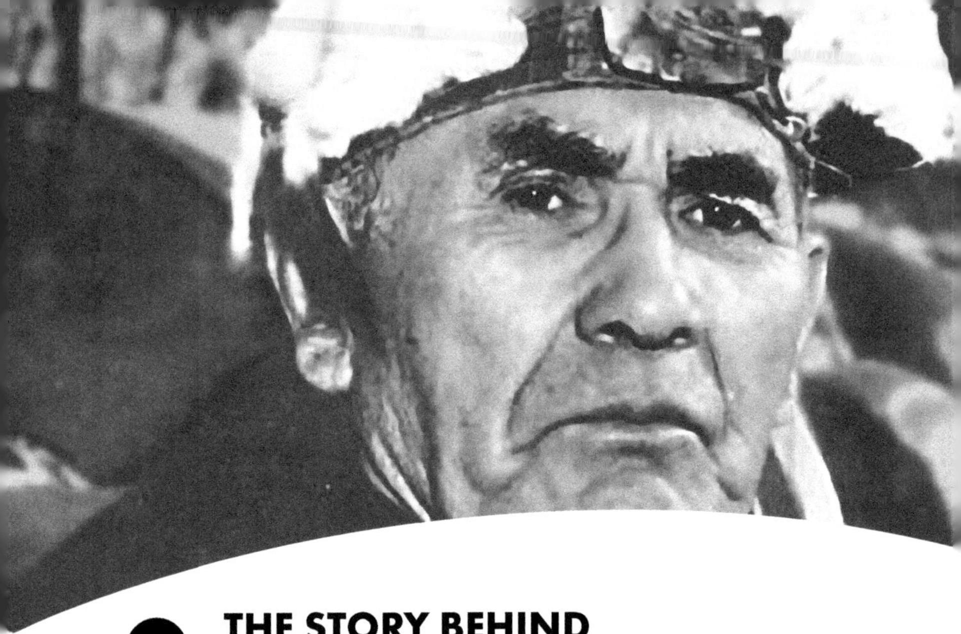

9 THE STORY BEHIND THAT TOTEM POLE

On Baseline Road there is a fading totem pole towering 60 feet above the traffic. It grandly sits in front of Scouts Canada's national headquarters.

I have no way of counting the number of times I have passed by this giant sentinel. I have no way of knowing how many people have done the same. One day I found myself thinking — all right, just what *is* the story on that totem pole?

Meet the Artist

The totem was carved in 1960 by Chief Mungo Martin of the Kwakiutl First Nation. He was assisted by his grandson Henry Hunt. Most of the carving was done in Victoria, B.C., near the ancestral home of the Kwakiutl and where Chief Martin was a prominent figure in

↑ Chief Mungo Martin
→ The totem pole he carved for the Boy Scouts of Canada.

Readers' Remarks

Traditionally, the poles are left to age and fade in place until they fall or rot away. Totems rarely last more than 60 or 80 years. But this one may last longer because it has been encased in cement at the bottom, preventing rot. The ageing of the pole represents the natural process of decay and death that happens with all living things. — *Denis*

I am crackers for the artwork of the Pacific Northwest! I have an interest in totem poles. So thank you for sharing this story. — *Urspo*

What a great story! I've passed it many times since the '80's and always wondered. — *Brianna*

The totem being hoisted on Baseline Road, 1961.

Northwest-Coast-Style aboriginal art.

The totem was gifted to Ottawa from the British Columbia Scouts, and cost approximately $8,000 to carve and paint. It is made from one BC cedar tree. The totem consists of six main figures; a Raven, a Man, a Grizzly Bear, a Cannibal Woman, a Killer Whale, and a Beaver. These are all clan crests from West Coast First Nations.

When it was completed the totem was transported on two railcars to Ottawa, where it was placed in front of the Scouts Canada building on Baseline. The totem's base is 10 feet long and was anchored in 75 tons of concrete.

The totem would be one of Chief Mungo Martin's last commissions. He died in 1962. His totems can be found around the world, including Windsor Great Park in the United Kingdom. That totem was a gift from the people of Canada to the Queen in June 1958.

The next time you pass this magnificent totem, think of the man who created it, and perhaps give a wave to the Great Spirit that Chief Martin believed lived within all his totems.

CANADA'S AIR FORCE ONE 10

On June 30, 1944, Canadian Forces Base Rockcliffe received a special aircraft — a B-24 bomber. It was built at the Consolidated Convair factory in Fort Worth, Texas and briefly in service with the United States Air Force. It came with serial number 44-1058.

But it was not bombs or troops that this B-24 was going to carry in Canada. The plane was going to carry Prime Minister Mackenzie King and other dignitaries. And although it would soon have the nickname "The Silver Saloon," the plane's official title was Royal Canadian Air Force One.

Which makes it the first plane in the world to carry the designation Air Force One.

Guess Where? Really?

In the United States — where the term Air Force One is now synonymous with the plane of the American president — the call signals Air Force One were not used until 1953. (Some of the earlier call signals for the place of the American president were more creative. Tried and rejected were *Guess Where, Guess Where II*, and *Sacred Cow*.)

Canada's Air Force One, although an historic plane, had short service and an inglorious end. The B-24 was modified in the summer of 1944, refitted with a VIP interior that could accommodate 10 passengers, and a separate office for King and his

Air Force One — renovated and ready for VIP duty, 1945. The emblem on Air Force One was the forerunner to the current RCAF logo. The roundel was used between 1945-1948..

Signing the United Nations Charter in San Francisco.

secretary. Windows were installed along each side of the fuselage and an extra side-door was installed, along with a galley kitchen and washroom.

A special, highly polished aluminum exterior finish and lightning bolt paint scheme were given to the PM's new plane. It was one of the first planes to sport the newly designed roundel on the fuselage (which later became the official RCAF symbol.) On August 30, 1944, Royal Canadian Air Force One was ready for service.

It was on Air Force One that Prime Minister Mackenzie King journeyed to San Francisco in June 1945 to help with the creation of the United Nations. The UN Charter was signed June 26, 1945 by representatives of 50 countries. Prime Minister Mackenzie King was

Air Force One — sold as a passenger plane 10 Air Chile.

Canada's signatory.

The plane later carried Governor General The Earl of Athlone and his family in March 1946, and then the Viscount Alexander of Tunis to Winnipeg, in September 1946.

In 1947 Air Force One carried General H. D. G. Crerar on tour of the Far East, a trip that included stops in Hawaii, Johnston Island, Kwajalein, Tokyo, and Nanking. King continued to use the plane as his VIP transport, but when he retired in 1948 the B-24 was flown from Ottawa to CFB Trenton, where it was put into storage.

Unused, and sitting in a Trenton hanger, the plane was sold as surplus to Chile in 1951. In Chile it was given a new paint scheme and operated under the Chilean designation "CC-CAN."

Landing in Santiago, Chile on February 21, 1955 the plane suffered a landing gear malfunction and skidded off the runway. It never flew again.

Four years later, in 1959, the plane was sold for scrap metal. Mackenzie King's Silver Saloon was no more, and the world's first Air Force One had disappeared into history.

Martes 22 de Febrero de 1955

Las Ultimas Noticias

Accidente. Ayer en Los Cerrillos

The last flight of Air Force One.

11 THE LEGEND OF *THE WISHING TREE*

When people are asked what best symbolizes Canada a common answer — maybe *the* most common answer — is a maple tree. Emblazoned on our national flag, and on federal government signage from sea to sea to sea, the maple tree and its leaf has the strongest claim to being Canada's national symbol, a crowded field with some worthy contenders. (Sorry beaver. Sorry moose.)

Our national symbol is strong and beautiful, but where is the world's oldest maple tree? Is it even *in* Canada? That question started me on a search that ended in Prince Edward County, where the world's oldest maple tree once grew.

The tree was felled in 1941, but there is not a maple tree in Ontario today that would be older, and it is quite possible there never was an older maple.

The Remarkable Story of a Remarkable Tree

History books tell us of the many important events that took place in the 13th-century, a list that ranges from the fierce invasion of China by Genghis Khan to the signing of the Magna Carta in England. Here in Canada, there was the exploration of the arctic region by Norse Vikings. It was also at this time — a story the history books missed somehow — that a maple tree began to grow.

That tree would become the oldest sugar maple in the world. And it was a well-known tree at one time, a tree that saw many local gatherings and important events take place beneath its boughs. And yes, it was a maple tree from Canada.

It was located near West Lake, in Prince Edward County, a magical area lined with blazing sand dunes, lapping waters and throngs of happy tourists every summer. Many of these visitors will drive along West Lake Road on their way to Sandbanks Provincial Park. Very few, if any, will realize they are driving over the remains of the world's oldest sugar maple, a tree once known around Prince Edward County as *The Wishing Tree.*

The tree got its name from the First Nations people who lived in the area. The sheer size of the tree made it a recognizable landmark and it was used for centuries to hold important meetings or barter for goods. It is said the Mohawks met under this tree to form their allegiance with the Iroquois League in the 1500s.

The wishing tree name came from a game young children used to play around the tree. They would collect fallen bark, then toss the bark into the dense, overhanging leaves. If the bark stayed in the tree, the child who threw it would be granted a wish.

When United Empire Loyalists arrived in Prince Edward County in the 1700s the well-trod footpath to the tree became a horse path.

The Wishing Tree in the1800s.

‚Then it was widened further to accommodate carriages, the settlers quickly coming to the same conclusion the Mohawk had reached centuries earlier — that tree was a good meeting place.

It was also, even then, an exceptional tree. It brought in curious visitors from across Upper Canada, many of whom would travel a day or more just to pace its circumference. Stare skywards and wonder how tall it might be.

(Several attempts were made in the 1800s to determine the tree's height — it was said by locals to be almost two-hundred-feet tall — but no scientific measurement of the tree's height was ever conducted.)

Postcards were made featuring the tree and in 1837 a lodge was build nearby, aptly named *Wishing Tree Lodge*. It was built on what is now West Lake Road. Sadly for our glorious tree (and you can contemplate the symbolism of this a long time) the advent of the automobile brought the demise of the tree.

Most people coming to see *The Wishing Tree* now drove cars, and the weight of the traffic irreversibly damaged the trees roots. To compound the problem in 1925 something happened to the tree that probably should have happened to a tree of that height centuries earlier — it got hit by lightening.

In 1941, after years of slow decay, the grand old tree was felled.

In Search of *The Wishing Tree*

So where was it?

No one in the area of West Lake Road seemed to have heard of the legend when I began knocking doors. But I soon found a resident who knew what I was talking about and she went inside her house to get a copy of a book called *A Settler's Dream*. Opening the book to page 126 I found the *Wishing Tree Lodge*, along with a short retelling of the wishing tree legend.

With this information, I was quickly able to confirm that the Wishing Tree Lodge was still there, although it is a private residence today. A Google Streetview also confirmed that this residence was the old brick lodge.

But where was the actual tree?

My parents told me about once seeing another book that had the legend of the Wishing Tree in it, along with a photo of an elderly

The Wishing Tree, as shown in a postcard marked Picton, Ontario.

gentleman who remembered the tree, and according to the photo caption, was standing on the exact spot where the tree once stood.

I soon found the book and photo, and to my delight I saw the old brick lodge in the background. I superimposed that photo over a current photo of the area, taken at the same angle, and there it was — the exact location of *The Wishing Tree.*

I drove right there. It's beneath a road now, but I was still able to stand on the spot where that magnificent tree grew. All around me smaller maple trees were growing, likely the offspring of the now vanished tree.

No plaque exists to mark the location. There are no indications anywhere of what a special place this once was — the place where the world's oldest and grandest maple tree once grew.

Now, for anyone reading who may think the legend of *The Wishing Tree* has been exaggerated in the retelling (That's all right. Scepticism is good) you can rest assured — it has not.

We may not know the height of the grand tree, but we know its age. The rings were counted after it was felled.

The Ontario Ministry of Natural Resources (MNR) says a maple tree near Peterborough has the oldest, verifiable age in the province. According to the MNR that tree is "at least 330 years old."

And what about *The Wishing Tree*? Well, when it was felled in 1941 and its inner rings counted, its age was found to be an astounding 731 years.

Which means Canada's grandest maple tree — if you want to do one last calculation — was around before the signing of the Magna Carta. Yes, I think a plaque would be nice.

12 THE OTTAWA RIVER'S MYSTERIOUS SOLAR WHEEL

Located in a dense forested area — at the confluence of the Ottawa and Carp rivers, at the foot of Chats Falls — lies a 400-ft diameter wheel aligned with the summer solstice.

Whether by coincidence or conscious effort, someone at some point in history has made a remarkable earthen wheel in what has always been a sacred and important place in the Ottawa Valley.

Further investigation into this "wheel" reveals interesting details that will either prove it to be of a more ancient origin, or perhaps merely a more modern construction that coincidentally aligns its axis with the setting sun on the summer solstice.

In order to learn more about the history of the summer solstice and its significance throughout history, we must travel back in time to the early Bronze Age.

History of the Solstice

The summer solstice has been significant to almost all cultures, observed and celebrated as a time of rebirth, and fertility. It is when the sun stays longest in the sky. Derived from Latin words, "sol" (sun) and "sistere" (to stand still). Solsistre. Or, as we know, it "Solstice."

In our current calendar, June 21st marks the day of the annual summer solstice. The Christian Church rebranded this special day, celebrated by the ancients through pagan ritual, as "St. John the Baptist Day," which occurs three days after the solstice event. This date's relevance harkens back to the pagan practice of sacrifice that occurred on the summer solstice. Stonehenge in the United Kingdom is aligned with the summer solstice and to this day thousands gather there to celebrate the dawn on the solstice.

Ancient cultures would arrange wood or stones or build earthen mounds in a circular form to coincide with the celestial rotation of the sun. In the Bronze Age, this circle of stones on the landscape would also be illustrated in carved stones with a circle divided into four quadrants, denoting the summer solstice, the fall equinox, the winter solstice and then the spring equinox

The Egyptians built their Great Pyramids in alignment with the equinox and solstice, as did many other cultures, including North American native cultures, which marked the passage of the sun and stars by way of medicine wheels.

→ The Goseck Circle in Germany has gates aligned with the solstice.
↘ Native American solar cross.
↓ Solar Cross petroglyph from Denmark.

The sun on summer solstice, setting between the pyramids Khufu and Khafr.

A Native American medicine wheel, tracking the movements of the moon and stars.

Medicine wheels marked the geographical directions and astronomical events of the sun, moon, some stars, and some planets in relation to the Earth's horizon at that location. These rock sites were also used for important ceremonies, teachings, and as sacred places to give thanks to the Creator, Gitchi Manitou or Great Spirit.

Is That a Wheel?

I first noticed what looks like an earthen wheel at the base of Chats falls while examining aerial imagery of the area. Chats Falls has been a place of importance to nomadic First Nations people for millennia. It was a place of both strategic importance — the falls were on the trading route that brought copper and other minerals from Lake Superior east along the Ottawa River, or Great River as it was known then — and spiritual importance — there is a burial ground nearby. So it would not be surprising if something had been built near Chats

Chats Falls as it looked before being damned in 1930 for a hydro station.

Falls, long ago, to mark the area's importance. I looked at my aerial photos and began to wonder.

The photos show a definite outline of something circular in the forest, where the Carp River meets the Ottawa River within Fitzroy Provincial Park. It is in the shape of a wheel, with spokes inside. Placing overlays of known "medicine wheels" and "Solar Cross" shapes, they do align with the sun's axis on the summer solstice.

I went to investigate. The area is situated in very dense forest, swampy and fern covered, a low-lying area that is likely flooded each spring. Wet, and damp, there is a definite mounding of earth to create four spokes that converge at a central mound "hub."

Another pronounced mound is noticeable on the western spoke edge. Using Sun Surveyor to calculate the position of the sun on the summer solstice, one of the spokes is aligned with the setting sun on the June 20-21st solstice event, if you were standing on the central

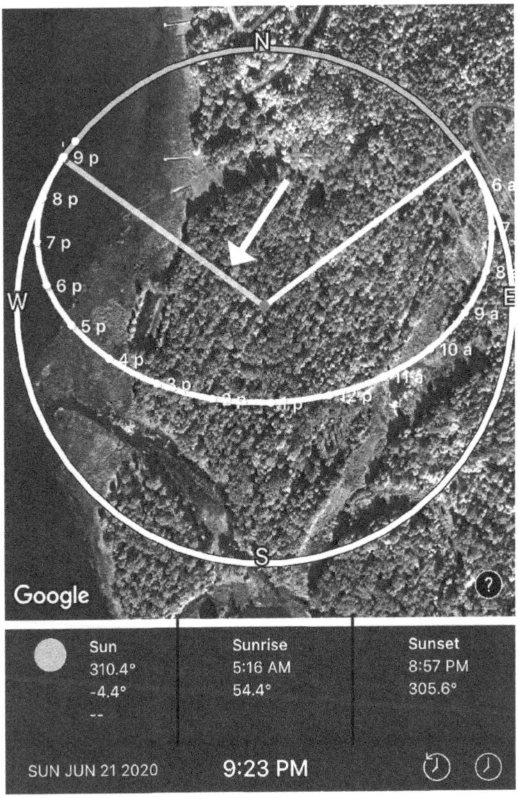

Sun Surveyor showing the axis of one spoke is in alignment with the setting sun on the Summer Solstice.

mound. It also matches known First Nation medicine wheels in orientation, and their inherent quadrants of celestial significance.

Also on the nearby shoreline there looks to be a stone weir, purpose unknown. Was this a native fishing camp and the stone weir was used to catch fish as they used to do centuries ago. Or is a modern park feature?

The whole structure is quite peculiar. There are piles of rocks that have been carefully placed in key positions around the wheel. Again, this is *dense* forest. I have no idea what else the formation could be, unless it is some park structure from decades ago that has overgrown since. It is quite inaccessible however, and with old growth trees everywhere, I don't know what could have been built there recently.

Perhaps someone reading knows more about this strange earthen wheel. At the moment all I can say with certainty is that there is a 400-ft diameter earthen-and-stone wheel on the shore of the Ottawa River at Chats Falls that lines up perfectly with the summer solstice.

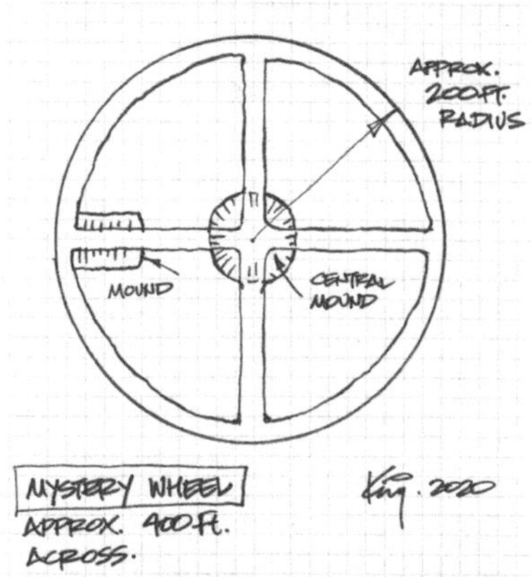

↑ An earthen mound is in the centre of the "wheel."
← My sketch of what the wheel would have looked like when first built.
↙ ↓ Most of the area is covered in ferns and tree saplings, making the wheel almost impossible to see, but there are some interesting piles of stones.

13 Ottawa's Forgotten Mega-Church

Lansdowne Park has hosted many events and seen many large gatherings over the years, from the mustering of troops in the Great War to Rolling Stones concerts not so long ago. Yet strangely, the largest event ever held at Lansdowne Park has been largely forgotten — The Marian Congress of 1947.

The Congress have been the largest event ever held in the city, let alone the civic park in the Glebe. Some estimates say as many as a million people took part in the Catholic celebration and pilgrimage to Ottawa that year. Which would have been four times the population of the city in 1947.

The Marian Congress was held in Ottawa to commemorate the 100th anniversary of the founding of the Archdiocese of Ottawa. It was held over six days and nights, with mass celebrated 24 hours a day. Priests began a new mass every half hour, conducted from the stage of a make-shift church built on the banks of the Rideau Canal.

Within Lansdowne, near the Aberdeen Pavilion, 15 confessional booths were made, and one hundred priests manned them. (News

Worshippers celebrate masses at the Marian Congress in 1947.

MARIAN CONGRESS REPOSITORY—His Excellency Most Rev. Alexandre Vachon is shown with the architect's model of the magnificent outdoor altar which has been erected at Lansdowne Park. Visitors to Ottawa this week may see the actual altar which is 550 feet long and 155 feet at the tower.

↑ The alter at the mega-church.
→ An architect's model of the structure.

reports of the day say the congress needed more of both.) The congress culminated with a radio address by Pope Pius XII and the consecration of the "Dominion of Canada to the Immaculate Heart of Mary" on June 22.

Taking part in Consecration Prayers that day were federal cabinet minister James J McCann, and future prime minister Louis St. Laurent. Bishops, priests and pilgrims came from 46 countries and by all accounts, Ottawa proved to be a perfect host city. Here is what Cardinal Pierre-Marie Gerlier, Achbishop of Lyon had to say about the 1947 Marian Congress:

"As Bishop of Lourdes for eight years, I have seen magnificent celebrations; Ottawa has surpassed them all. ... It will not be possible, from now on, to evoke feasts in honour of the Blessed Virgin without recalling the name of Ottawa."

And aerial view massive monument built on the edge of the Rideau canal at Lansdowne.

What Happened to the Mega-church?

To accommodate all those who attended the Marian Congress of 1947, one of the largest structures ever built in Ottawa went up by the banks of the Rideau Canal, a "mega-church" that looks like it would have rivalled the megalithic architecture of German architect Albert Speer.

The church had a 500-foot stage and seating for 75,000 people. On this stage, the Dionne Quintuplets sang for the assembled pilgrims and clergy. Behind it, on the evening of Consecration Prayers, the largest fireworks display in North America (until that time) exploded in the skies overhead.

The church was constructed by Ottawa contractors Collet Freres Ltd. and was painted in the colours of the Blessed Virgin Mary — white and blue. Photographs show a structure that probably out-did Speer in terms of grandeur and spectacle.

It was still a make-shift church, though, constructed for the six-day event and taken down right afterwards. There seems to be no trace of the church anywhere in the city. (Lansdowne Park itself has mostly vanished. The Aberdeen Pavilion is the only building remaining that would have been used during the 1947 Marian Congress.)

Indeed, were it not for a short film about the congress shot by Father Maurice Proulx, and later posted on-line by Ottawa diocese member Dennis Girard, the event may be completely forgotten today.

The statue of the Blessed Virgin Mary, now permanently installed at Blessed Sacrament Parish in Ottawa.

When Girard discovered Father Proulx' film, he was astounded to learn about the Marian Congress. He was a devout catholic, born and raised in Ottawa, and had never heard of the event. He set off on a pilgrimage of his own shortly afterwards, to find out everything he could about the 1947 Marian Congress.

That brought him to Cap-de-la-Madeleine a few years ago, where he was able to track down one item from that long-forgotten mega-church. The statue of Mary venerated in Ottawa as part of the congress was there in an Oblate seminary.

The Oblates gifted Girard the pilgrim statue and it was installed permanently at Blessed Sacrament Parish in Ottawa on Mother's Day, 2017.

This is the only item I could find, still with us, from the largest church ever built in Ottawa

Readers' Remarks

I had never heard of this event nor the church. It is not part of the history of the city at all. That is unfortunate it could add elements to any visit to the city. — *Larry*

What an amazing piece of Ottawa's history. In fact, a part of Canada's history. — *Carol*

I was there. I was 14 years old. Will never forget it. it was incredible. — Norman

Remember hearing about it in my youth on Muriel Street in the 40s and 60s. — *Ken*

14 FIRST STORE IN THE VALLEY

About 57 kilometres northwest of Ottawa, a nondescript piece of property near Chats Falls and Quyon on the Ottawa River is part of the oldest known permanent European structure in the Ottawa Valley. Concealed under the cover of bushes, the original stone foundation of a structure is visible. This is most likely the remains of a home built in the late 18th century that later became a busy trading post.

A Popular Route

Situated in an area that nomadic Indigenous people had used for thousands of years to transport goods and copper from Lake Superior east along the Ottawa River, this parcel of land was an important strategic and cultural piece of property. French *voyageurs* and *coureurs des bois* later used the same transit route; Samuel Champlain would have passed by this site in the early 1600s.

However, it wouldn't be until 1786 that Joseph Mondion would build a permanent residence here on what is now called Mondion Point — 14 years before Philemon Wright arrived from Massachusetts to settle in what is now the Hull sector of Gatineau.

↑ A typical Hudson's Bay Trading Post in the 1800's.

Thence to Mondion's Point in Onslow is but a short distance; and here is seen one of the original North-West posts, established on the Ottawa at the most flourishing period of that company's existence. The dwelling-house and store bear evidence of their antiquity from the dilapidated state they are in, and the soil is too poor about the point to invite the resident agent to the culture of the farm. Mr. Thomas resides here as agent for the Hudson's Bay Company, for whom he keeps a store supplied with the articles most in demand by the Indians and other traders, such as broad cloths, blankets, beads, ammunition, spirits, &c. Nearly opposite Mondion's Point, at the other extremity of the line of the falls, is Mr. Sheriff's settlement and residence, in the township of Huntly, U.C.

The British Dominions in North America by Joseph Bouchette, 1832.

Traders of Many Types

A wise entrepreneur, Mondion raised cattle and hogs and sold meat to the hungry fur traders passing by and portaging Chats Falls. He operated his little trading empire on the Ottawa River until he was apparently shut down for selling illegal whisky. Packing up shop in 1800, he sold his piece of property to Forsyth, Richardson and Company, a trading company from Montreal. In 1804, the North West Company of Montreal took over the property.

In 1821, the British government forced the North West Company and Hudson's Bay Company to merge, in an effort to end the often-violent competition between the two trading companies, and the piece of land became an official Hudson's Bay trading post. This once-remote outpost consisted of log cabins and wooden storehouse filled with inventory, such as guns, blankets, iron tools and clothing.

Readers' Remarks

I can add a little bit about the history of Mondion Point. I cannot immediately cite a reference but I have come across information in the past where Mondion may have been Metis.

From at least 1808 to 1812, the property was operated as both a farm and trading post by a Mr. Cameron, possibly still under the ownership of the Northwest Company or Forsyth Richardson. In February of 1812, John McNab (Sr.) visited Mr. Cameron en-route from Moose Fort to Montreal, New York and London. McNab described the farmstead as consisting of a house, a large barn and a yard for cattle, hogs and poultry. The yard was surrounded by open sheds and railings. — *Ross*

Just a note about the neighbouring lots. Ranges 1-6 (some 12,000 acres) were owned by Philemon Wright, and somewhere on those lots he built a house and barns. The exact location of the house is apparently lost in history (something next for you to find?) — *Rick*

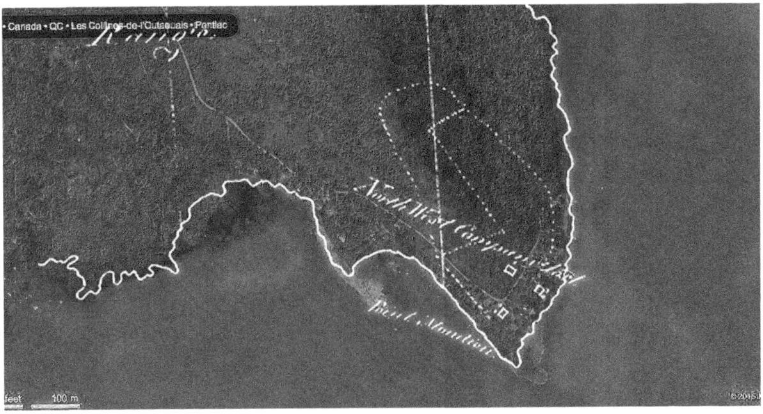

↑ A Bing Map of the Chats Falls area, first overlaid with an 1805 map.
→ Then overlaid with an 1845 map.
↓ A sketch below shows where I found the stone ruins, in relation to the two maps.

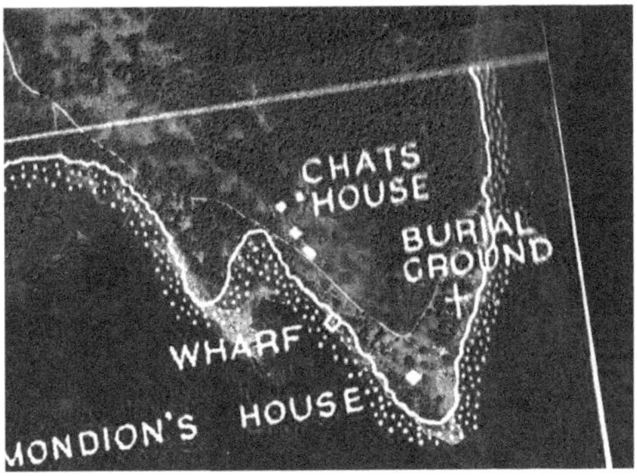

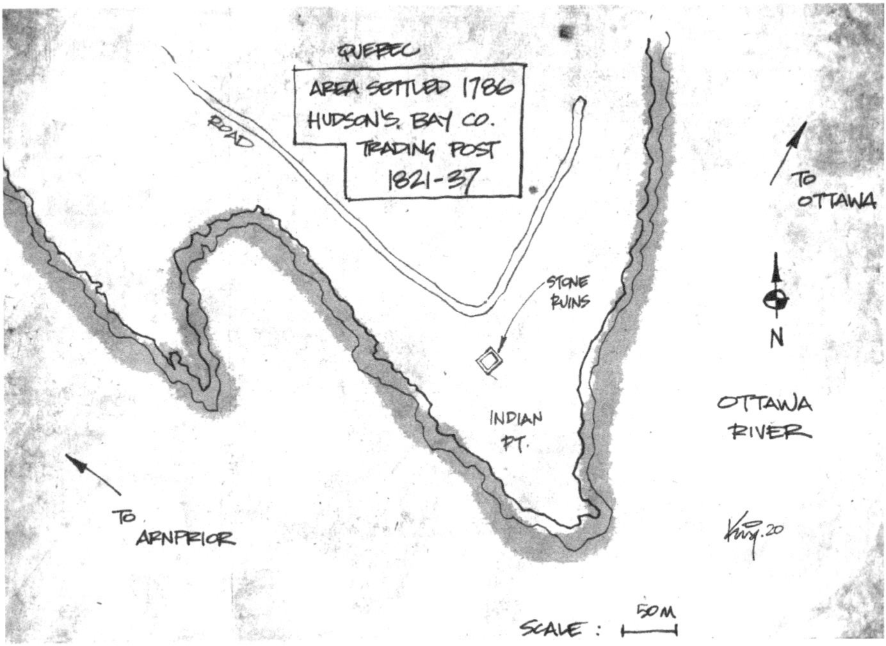

In 1837, the trading post was abandoned, since most of the Indigenous population had been displaced. The fur trade was coming to an end, with lumber being the new commodity along the Ottawa River. The log cabins fell into ruin and the land was transformed into farmland. It later became cottage country, which it remains today.

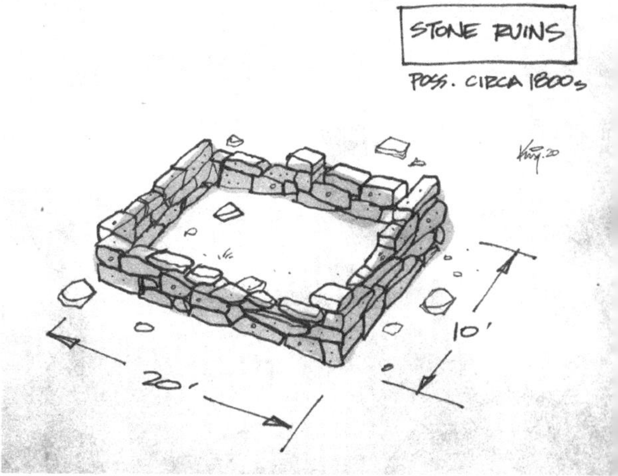

A sketch of the stone ruins.

The stone ruins, as I found them.

Finding the Site

To locate this once-prosperous trading post, I referred to an 1805 North West Company map, which shows where the original structures were. Transposing that map on a current aerial map indicated where the ruins may lie today.

Of course, the original plot of land settled by Mondion and used by the Hudson's Bay Company has been subdivided into many lots since they departed. However, a significant parcel of waterfront land that Mondion and the Hudson's Bay Company once owned is still undeveloped. Nearby, off the main road, some overgrown stone foundations remain, likely those of the original 1786 Mondion house and the 1800s trading post.

I find it seriously disheartening that such an important piece of Ottawa Valley history, if not Canadian history, remains forgotten. Who knows what important historical artifacts lie beneath this land? The federal or provincial government should preserve these ruins and recognize them for their cultural and historical value to this country.

15 THE FIRST SHIP ON THE GREAT LAKES

The Great Lakes are the largest group of freshwater lakes on Earth, a vast network of in-land lakes draining to the Atlantic Ocean, via the St. Lawrence River. The lakes have been traversed for millennia, going back to dug-out canoes that were used 12,000 years ago.

It would not be until the 17th century, though, that the Great Lakes would first see a sailing vessel. History books tell us a French brigantine, or *barque* ,called *Le Griffon* commissioned by René-Robert Cavelier, Sieur de La Salle, was built on the Niagara River.

Le Griffon would be labelled the first sailing vessel to travel the Great Lakes, in the year 1679. However, *Le Griffon* disappeared on its maiden voyage and has never been found. It is considered the Holy Grail of Great Lakes shipwrecks.

Yet after researching old documents and notes from the 1600's, I now believe that *Le Griffon* was not the first, but actually the fifth sailing vessel on the Great Lakes..

The Legend of *Le Griffon*

In July of 1673 Louis de Buade, Comte de Frontenac et de Palluau, better known as Count Frontenac, Governor of New France, traveled to a place called "Cataraqui", where the river that bears that name,

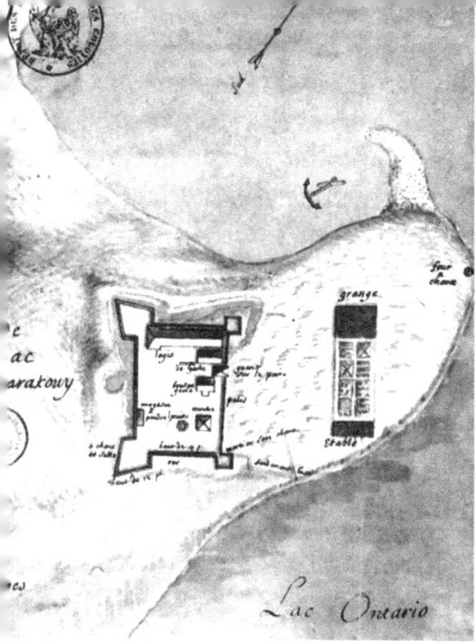

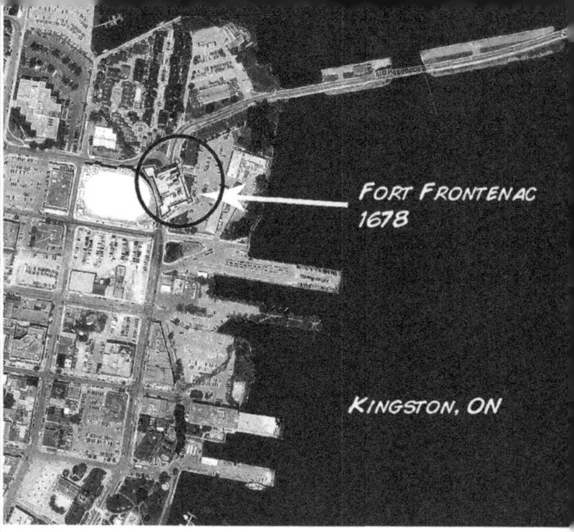

← 1685 map shows Fort Frontenac.
↑ Fort Frontenac ghosted over by present-day Kingston.

and the St. Lawrence River, meet at the eastern end of Lake Ontario. This spot is now Kingston

Under the advice of explorer and fur trader René-Robert Cavelier, Sieur de La Salle, this spot was chosen to build a French fort. La Salle started building the fort in 1673, along with a harbour to contain a future fleet of sailing vessels.

It was here, in this Kingston harbour, that it seems the very first sailing vessel on the Great Lakes was constructed and launched. I found this in my research of a document titled *"Lettre de Frontenac au Ministre,"* dated November 13th, 1673, in which Frontenac himself mentions:

"... with the aid of a vessel now building, will command Lake Ontario, keep peace with the Iroquois, and cut off the trade with the English." The letter then continues to state that *"with another vessel on Lake Erie, we, the French, can command all the Upper Lakes."*

Frontenac's letter pre-dates the *Griffon* by six years. If it were just one letter, and no other evidence, the *Griffon* could probably keep its claim to being the first sailing vessel on the Great Lakes. But it's *not* just one letter. A 1677 letter from Frontenac also states that: *"Four vessels, of from twenty-five to forty tons, had been built for the lake and the river."*

The first ship built by LaSalle at Fort Frontenac — now the intersection of Ontario Street and Barrack Street in Kingston — would have been the Great Lakes' first sailing vessel (if you don't believe the theory that Vikings had already ventured down the St. Lawrence River 600 years earlier.)

LEFT FORT FRONTENAC NOV. 18TH 1678
W/ LAMOTTE AND HENNEPIN
TO NIAGARA TO BEGIN BUILDING "LE GRIFFON"
"FRONTENAC"
10 TONNES
BUILT 1676-77
AT FORT FRONTENAC (KINGSTON)

This first boat was called *Le Frontenac* after the Governor of New France and was a sloop-type vessel of about 10 tonnes, with a single mast. It would be this vessel that would carry two men to Niagara where they would establish a construction site to build *Le Griffon.*

Of the four sailing vessels that were recorded as being harboured at Fort Frontenac in 1677, one was the sloop *Frontenac,* with another being recorded as a bigger vessel of about 40 tonnes, likely a ketch, that was used as the supply ship for *Le Griffon.*

It was this second vessel that carried LaSalle and his companion Henri de Tonti to Niagara. So, what happened to these first ships? *Le Griffon* gets all the attention, but it was *Le Frontenac* and the unnamed ketch that were actually the first ships to sail the Great Lakes. Has anyone looked for them?

Before *Le Griffon* — *Le Frontenac*

It was a cold November day in 1678 when LaSalle sent his comrades Dominiqued LaMotte and Louis Hennepin aboard *Le Frontenac* to find a suitable spot to build and launch *Le Griffon* above Niagara Falls. They departed November 18th, 1678 encountering high winds and staying close to the north shore of Lake Ontario.

It is likely that they stopped for overnight moorage in many of the bays along the way, including Port Hope, before reaching the native village of Taiaiagnon on November 26th, at the mouth of the Humber River near present day Mississauga.

Here they sought refuge from the cold and were welcomed by the residents of Taiaiagnon. *Le Frontenac* was soon locked in ice however, and the sailors had to cut and chip their way out of the bay before sailing to the mouth of the Niagara River on December 6th.

"UNKNOWN NAME" APPROX. 40TONNES
BUILT IN 1673-77
AT FORT FRONTENAC (KINGSTON)
LEFT W/LASALLE & TONTI
DEC.24TH 1678 FOR NIAGARA W/
SUPPLIES TO BUILD 'LE GRIFFON'
ANCHORS, CORDS, HARDWARE ETC.
WRECKED ON SOUTH SHORE OF LAKE ONTARIO JAN.8TH 1679
SOMEWHERE NEAR 30 MILE POINT LIGHTHOUSE. WRECK NEVER FOUND.

Once there, they dragged Le *Frontenac* ashore to keep it from getting frozen again in the ice and set out to find a spot to build *Le Griffon*. Later that month, on Christmas Eve of 1678, LaSalle and Tonti boarded the ketch at Fort Frontenac — filled with anchors, cannons, cords, sails, hardware and other supplies needed to build *Le Griffon* — and set out for the Niagara River.

It was not a good voyage. The winds were fierce, and the ship was almost bashed apart somewhere off Prince Edward County, likely

A late 1600s map showing the various locations the ships visited on their journey.

Hurons
du Petun
Kente
LAC FRONTENAC
OU
ONTARIO

around Point Traverse. On Christmas Day, LaSalle and Tonti crossed Lake Ontario to arrive at what is now Rochester, NY. They sailed along the southern coast of Lake Ontario, stopping at a Seneca village.

Here, LaSalle and Tonti decided to carry on by foot to meet LaMotte at Niagara. Their vessel was left in charge of its pilot and crew, but they did not secure it well enough and on January 8th a wind carried away the supply laden boat, carrying it fifteen kilometres west until it broke apart near Thirty-Mile Point. A messenger was sent to tell LaSalle his ship had been wrecked, and he hurried back.

Lasalle managed to salvage some anchors and chains but the ship and most of its supplies and provisions were lost. This would make LaSalle's ketch the first shipwreck in the Great Lakes, one year *before* the loss of *Le Griffon*.

LaSalle and his men dragged what they could salvage from the wrecked ship fifty kilometres overland to the Niagara construction site (which is now Griffon Park in Niagara Falls.) After laying *Le Griffon*'s keel on January 26th, 1679, and driving the first bolt into it, LaSalle left the operation in charge of Tonti and arrived back to Fort Frontenac after a 400-kilmetre dead-of-winter hike through the woods that nearly killed him.

What Happened Next?

LaSalle's men continued to build *Le Griffon* throughout the winter of 1678, but were met with cold temperatures, disgruntled workers, hostile bands of Senaca and the constant threat of sabotage. Tonti made sure to launch ahead of schedule and get out of there as quickly as possible, with *Le Griffon* hitting the water with great ceremony in early summer of 1679. It would be the *largest* sailing vessel on the Great Lakes when launched, but not the first, as some will have us believe.

Tonti towed *Le Griffon* through the turbulent waters of the Niagara River to Lake Erie, before LaSalle climbed aboard, unfurled its sails and steered into the lake on August 7th, 1679. Outfitted with seven cannons, two of which were brass, *Le Griffon* now sailed the unchartered Great Lakes and headed for Green Bay, Wisconsin, where LaSalle got off the vessel to explore Lake Michigan with a party of four canoes.

An early 1700s illustration of the construction of *LeGriffon* in 1679

La Salle ordered *Le Griffon* to off-load merchandise for him at Mackinac Island, and then on September 18th, the pilot and crew of five left either Rock Island or Washington Island for its return voyage to the Niagara River, its cargo hold filled with valuable furs.

Le Griffon was never seen again. Its final whereabouts is one of the greatest maritime mysteries of all time. Some say the crew took the furs and burned the ship. Others say it went down in a storm. But no one knows.

While *Le Griffon* has become a maritime legend, almost no attention has been given to what would have been the first sailing vessel on the Great Lakes — Lasalle's unnamed ketch. That ship was lost off 30 Mile Point in 1678.

Yes, it would be great to find *Le Griffon*, but wouldn't it be just as interesting to find the first ship? At least we know — unlike *Le Griffon* — the general vicinity of where that wreck may lie. It awaits discovery, 342 years after it went down.

Cconstruction site of *Le Griffon* in 1679

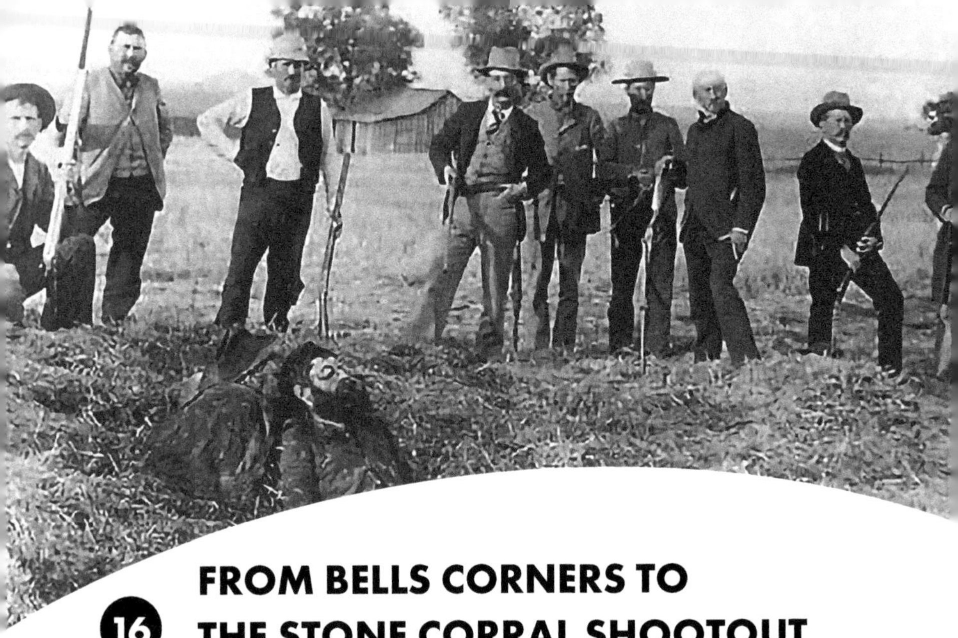

16 FROM BELLS CORNERS TO THE STONE CORRAL SHOOTOUT

On Greenbank Road South of Hunt Club, in the Greenbelt, a flat parcel of NCC-owned land stretches west toward Cedarview Road. Nothing marks its place in history as the childhood home of Chris Evans.

And why might an historical marker be appropriate for such a place? Well, without knowing the actual number, I would think there are few markers in Canada showing the birthplace of anyone involved in a legendary Old West gunfight.

And Chris Evans, born just off Cedarview Road, would be someone who would qualify for such a marker.

Moving to California

Bells Corners residents Thomas and Mary Ann Evans brought their son Chris into the world on this land on February 19, 1847. Young Chris worked on his parents' farm

↑ John Sontag and the posse that shot him.
→ Mary Ann and Thomas Evans.

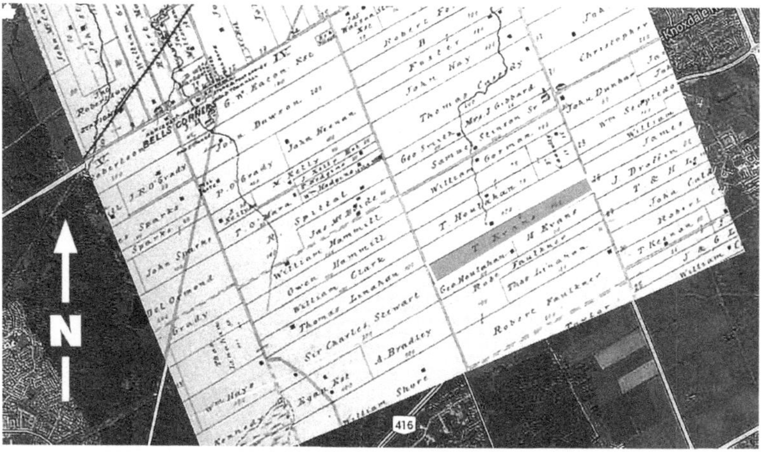

An 1880 concession map of Bells Corners shows where Chris Evans would have grown up.

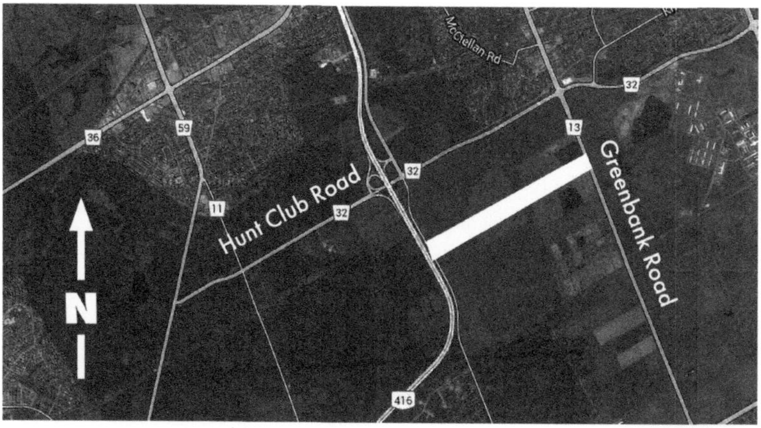

Goggle Maps shows where the Evans' farm would have been.

The old farm is now party of the Greenbelt and owned by the National Capital Commission.

George Custer, Evans' commander.

Molly Evan.

until the age of 16, when he decided to seek his fortune. He headed south and soon joined the Union Army fighting against the Confederate forces in the U.S. Civil War.

A natural sharpshooter, he stayed with the Army after the war as a talented scout and served alongside American legend Lieutenant-Colonel George Custer of Custer's Last Stand fame. However, Evans later deserted the Army, heading to California and the emerging Wild West. Once in California, he met and married Molly Byrd, and settled down on a farm in Visalia.

There, in the quiet hills of the San Joaquin Valley, Evans worked as a miner, teamster, lumberjack and railroad employee. To work on his farm, he hired a young man named John Sontag, who also worked with the Southern Pacific Railroad. After Sontag was injured on the job, the railroad fired him.

Evans and Sontag became close friends, even going into a livery business together in Modesto, California. Like many in the area, they shared a dislike of the Southern Pacific Railroad, since the company expropriated many properties under market value.

And then . . . Some Train Robberies

A fire burned down their Modesto business in 1891, leaving them both bankrupt and forcing them to return to Visalia. Around this time, an unusual number of train robberies occurred, perpetrated by two masked men.

On August 3, 1892, two bandits held up a Southern Pacific Railroad train near Fresno and made off with $50,000. Authorities followed the robbers' tracks to Visalia and paid a visit to the Evans farm. Two men — railroad detective Will Smith and deputy sheriff George Witt — approached the Evans residence.

Evans and Sontag appeared with shotguns and a firefight erupted. Evans and Sontag blasted their way out, wounding both lawmen and killing another who arrived had on the scene. Thus began what was the largest manhunt in California history.

An enormous posse hunted Evans and Sontag.

Who Are Those Guys?

Dozens of lawmen, 300 armed civilians and a score of bounty hunters wanted to claim the $10,000 reward for the pair's capture, dead or alive. However, locals provided the well-liked pair with cover and hiding places, meaning Evans and Sontag were able to avoid any confrontation for about a month. Then, one day in September, a posse tracked Evans and Sontag to a cabin in the mountains.

Evan and Sontag quickly ambushed their pursuers, blowing out the cabin's windows, and killing a marshal and another member of the posse. After an eight-hour shootout, the wanted men escaped further into the mountains, where they spent the winter camping.

In the spring of 1893, a small posse of lawmen led by a new marshal, George E. Gard, stealthily tracked the fugitives and gathered information. Gard soon got a tip that Sontag and Evans were planning to visit Evans's wife, Molly, at the Evans cabin, about 10 miles northeast of Visalia. Gard and his posse headed to the Stone Corral, next to the Evans home, so they could begin searching the area.

The Stone Corral Shootout

Once at the Stone Corral, Gard and his men — Hiram Lee Rapelje, a deputized bounty hunter; Fred Jackson, a policeman from Nevada; and Thomas Burns — holed up in a cabin to see whether Evans and Sontag would pass by. The tip would prove correct. On June 11, 1893, Evans and Sontag appeared on the hill overlooking the Stone Corral. Evans wanted to fire a few shots into the cabin below to see whether anybody was there, but because the place appeared to be empty and

My sketches depicting the epic gunfight at the Stone Corral. Initials of the characters shown.

because the cabin was known as a "lovers' rendezvous," Sontag talked him out of it.

The two men got off their horses and headed down to the cabin where Jackson, the policeman, was keeping watch. Beside a haystack, Evans looked down and saw someone in the cabin window, and quickly opened fire with his Winchester rifle.

Hearing the shots, Jackson picked up his shotgun from the porch and blasted the pair, hitting Evans.

Knowing they were now being ambushed, the two retreated behind the haystack, lying as flat as possible to avoid the incoming fire from the cabin below.

The *San Francisco Examiner* later interviewed Rapelje, who said he'd agreed to take Sontag while Jackson took Evans. "But before I had time to get a line on Sontag's breast, Fred fired. Evans fell endway, with both hands up. Sontag dived for the straw pile, and I let go as [sic] him. Then both of them, from behind the strawstack, turned loose their big Winchesters. Bullets whizzed through the house."

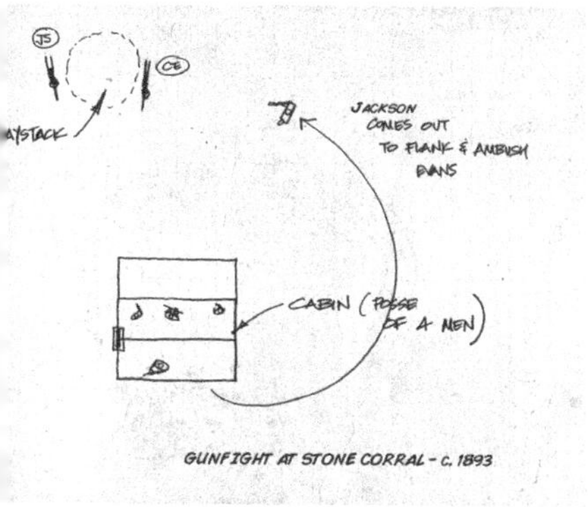

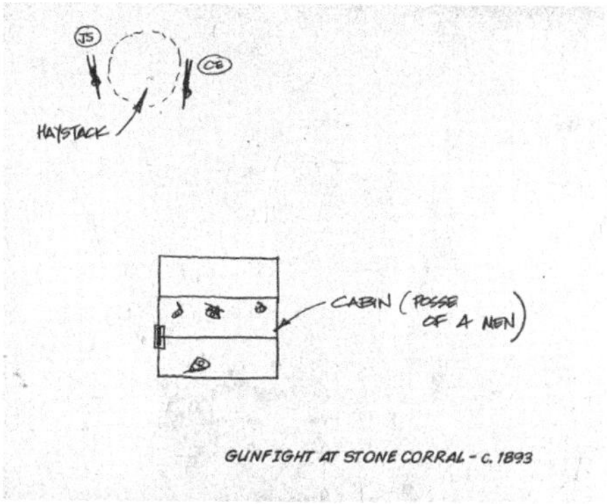

These sketches show the cabin where the ambush was planned.

Enraged at the ambush, Evans and Sontag fired a barrage of angry shots into the cabin. Jackson ran out the cabin and approached the haystack from the side, but Evans caught sight of the approaching policeman and blasted him with his revolver, taking out Jackson's kneecaps and legs. At some point, Sontag was hit in the stomach and in the right arm, taking him out of the battle. As night fell, the adversaries lost visibility.

A Dying Friend

Now dying, Sontag pleaded with Evans to shoot him and then escape in the dark. Evans initially refused both requests but eventually grabbed his rifle and began to crawl away from the haystack. Rapelje spotted him and opened fire, hitting him in the face and arm. Evans did not shoot back but managed to escape.

Left for dead, Sontag raised his own revolver to his head in an effort to end his misery but the gun missed, injuring the dying outlaw even more. The men in the cabin ignored Sontag's shouted pleas for water and stayed inside until dawn, when reinforcements arrived. Together, they rushed the haystack and found Sontag

The infamous haystack, where the posse photographed a dying John Sontag.

lying there, barely alive. When a reporter arrived, the posse heaved up Sontag's almost-lifeless body for a photograph, which would soon appear in the *San Francisco Examiner*. Then Sontag was hauled away on a wagon to a jail cell in Visalia.

Evans Heads to Jail

Meanwhile, Evans — although badly wounded — walked six miles up Wilcox Canyon to another cabin and begged the owners for help. They bandaged him up but, a few days later, informed the police they had a fugitive in their cabin.

A large force of lawmen surrounded the cabin, expecting another massive shootout, but Evans surrendered without resistance. He was taken to the jail in Visalia and put in the cell next to Sontag, who would die of his wounds in jail on July 3. As for Evans, his left arm had to be amputated, and he lost his right eye. On December 13, 1893, after a trial in Fresno, he was sentenced to life in Folsom Prison.

Chris Evans shortly after his capture.

Despite the lack of an arm and an eye, Evans escaped from the Fresno jail with a fellow prisoner on December 28, leaving Marshal John D. Morgan wounded. Once again, the Ottawa native returned to Visalia to see his wife and children, where he was captured again without incident. Evans was then sent to Folsom and remained until May 1911, when he was released under condition he never return to California again.

And into the Sunset

With his wife and family, Evans moved to Portland, Oregon, where he read, and tended to his garden and cats, living out his remaining days without incident.

Evans claimed that he never did rob a train and that he only ever fired his gun in self-defence, stating, "I am guilty of no crimes. I killed men who were trying to kill me." The boy from Bells Corners died in 1917 and is buried in Mount Calvary Cemetery in Portland, Oregon.

An elderly Chris Evans in Portland, Oregon.

His parents, Tom and Mary Ann, died in 1898 and 1893, respectively, and their graves can still be seen today in the Union Cemetery in Bells Corners. Chris Evans's wife, Molly, would spend her last days in Laguna Beach, California, where she died in 1944.

The Wild West is full of characters, most notably those who lived a life of crime. The era of the Hollywood Western peaked in the 1960s and 1970s, but I still eagerly await the movie that should be made about the Outlaw from Bells Corners.

↑ The gravestone of Christopher Evans.
→ That of his parents, Thomas and Mary Evans

17 GHOST TRAIN TO THE AIRPORT

When the Ottawa Airport was a World War II training base, it was called Uplands Air Base, or No. 8 Service Flying Training School.

Uplands was where pilots came to be trained for war service, but when World War II ended the airbase became home to the jet age with CF-86 Sabre fighter jets stationed there, along with many other military aircraft. This called for a massive expansion of the old airbase, which needed new runways and hangers to accommodate the jets.

This was a large construction job and materials had to be brought in on a massive scale. To solve the anticipated transportation problems of getting the material there a spur line from the existing Canadian

The aerial photo above shows where the spur line to the airport would have been, back in the '50s.

Pacific rail line was built. The spur line allowed material for the new airport to be shipped directly from the ports in Prescott, on the St. Lawrence River.

This 1950s spur line curved west from the CP line and crossed the current Airport Parkway where it ended by the airport hangers. The new rail line stayed operational after the airport expansion, transporting munitions, equipment and other material during the busy Cold War days of Uplands Air Force Base.

The rail line later fell into disuse, and when Uplands was closed the tracks were removed and the line shut, but remnants of the gravel bed are still there, as you can see in these photos.

The gravel beds harken back to a time when rail service in Ottawa actually, what's the word I'm looking for . . .worked. I wish we could bring back that ghost train to the airport.

Although I suppose one can argue there's a fair number of ghost trains in Ottawa already these days.

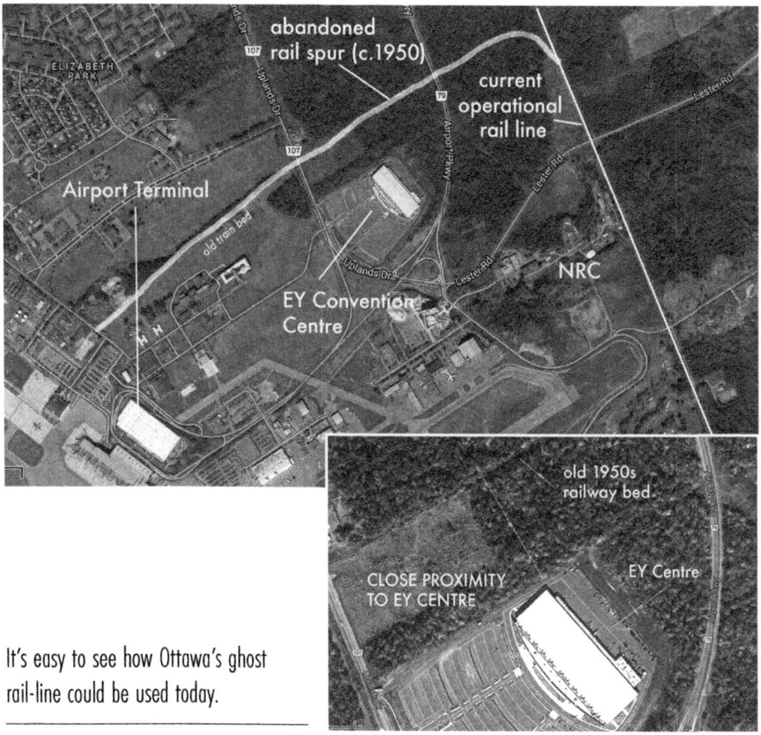

It's easy to see how Ottawa's ghost rail-line could be used today.

18 THE LAST ZELLERS

The last Zellers store in Canada closed in 2020.

If that sentence surprises you — wasn't Zellers already gone? — relax, you didn't miss anything. There were only two Zellers left in Canada when they both closed on the same day in 2020.

One of them just happened to be in Bells Corners.

When the Lowest Price Was the Law

Zellers was once a retail giant in Canada. Founded in 1931, the company reached its peak in 1999, when there were 350 Zellers stores across the country. Those were heady times for the company, but trouble had already arrived.

Walmart came to Canada in 1994.

Within ten years of Walmart arriving, Zellers had started shuttering stores. Seven years later, in 2011, the 80-year-old company surrendered, selling what was left of its retail empire to Minneapolis-based Target.

As conditions of that sale, Zellers was allowed to sublease some of its existing stores and stay in business until the end of March 2013. At that time, 100-150 of the remaining stores would reopen as Target outlets.

Although wildly successful in the United States, Target was somewhat less successful — just a smidgen — in Canada. In 2015, two years after its high-profile entry into Canada, Target closed all its Canadian stores.

That's a lot of corporate activity in 16 years (from the highs of 1999 to the utter debacle of 2015) and somewhere in that confusion someone forgot to kill off two Zellers stores.

A Sad Demise

Ah, wouldn't that have been a lovely story?

The truth — as anyone who visited the Bells Corners Zellers store in its last years would know — was that the last two Zellers stores were primarily liquidation outlets for parent company Hudson's Bay, which had acquired full ownership of Zellers in 1981.

So the store in Bells Corners was never quite the store I loved back in the '70s and '80s, when I would save up my paper-route money to buy an Atari2600 for $99.99 (on rain check) and countless bikes, clothes and toys.

But the signage in Bells Corners was all Zellers — *only you'll know how little you paid* — along with the displays, cash registers and shopping baskets.

With camera in hand I visited one of Canada's last Zellers stores before it closed. For one last stroll through the aisles of my youth.

The Zellers sign in Bells Corners is actually put overtop an even older Kmart sign. There was a Kmart location in Bells Corners until the 1990s when Zellers took over, with the familiar aisles and signage of my youth.

Readers' Remarks

As a Lynwood kid I also have many memories, but much more of K-Mart than Zellers. Oddly, I was driving by there recently and the sign jumped out at me. "Is that still open?" I thought. And then the thought passed. Until my question was answered by you. — *Dwight*

I have a vague memory from my youth of traveling to Canada and seeing the signs for Zellers, and being intrigued by it. It had a "Z" and it wasn't in the States. — *Urspo*

K-Mart had this rolling gizmo that looked like a poor-man's Dalek topped with a snowplow light. They moved that contraption all over the store and would announce random specials that lasted 15 minutes, while the light was flashing/spinning to guide savvy customers to a great deal. "Look for the flashing blue light," was how they announced it. — *Half Centennial*

↑ The familiar red plastic shopping baskets.
↓ The creepy mannequins of my 1980s youth.

↑ Lots of fluorescent lights. Love it.
↓ Love these old chrome metal sign stands.

CANADA'S CURSED CANDY KISS 19

It's available only in Canada. Only at Halloween. No one ever admits to liking it. Yet mysteriously it sells out each year.

The love-hate relationship Canadians have with Kerr's candy kiss is much like the relationship we have with winter — perplexing, annual, but apparently part of our identity.

Kerr's is a Canadian company. It went into business in St. Thomas, Ontario in 1895, founded by brothers Edward and Albert Kerr, recently emigrated from Scotland. There, the molasses candy kiss was a popular sweet, made primarily by Stewart and Young in Glasgow and sold under the name Steamship.

Kerr's would use that Scottish heritage in its branding — a highly recognizable Scottish tartan packaging that was used on all its candies. It was not until 1940, though, that the company would take a stab at replicating the molasses candy kisses so popular in Scotland.

So What Exactly Is It?

The ingredients in a Kerr's candy kiss wouldn't seem to add up to most-hated-candy status. The candy is made of blackstrap molasses (minimum 10 per cent), corn syrup, coconut oil, salt, cotton stearine, mono and diglycerides, soy lecithin and artificial flavour.

The last five ingredients don't exactly whet the appetite, but look at any ingredient box for any candy and you'll see the candy kiss is hardly an outlier.

So why does this candy top annual Halloween polls looking for the treat Canadians least want to find in their trick-and-treat bags?

Even Kerr's admits its own polling shows half their employees hate the stuff.

It also says production of the candy kiss has increased each year since it was introduced. Eighty years of steadily climbing sales. For a candy no one likes.

They're Making It Up

One reason given for the candy's popularity is nostalgia, a longing for a time when there wasn't any good candy. Or maybe there is some candy cult out there that has brainwashed people into liking the candy kiss; a cult similar to the one that must brainwash people into thinking Thrills gum doesn't taste like soap.

The earliest North American mention I could find of a molasses candy kiss was in an 1887 edition of the *Official White House Cook Book*. It was listed under *Dessert Candy*. American molasses candy had different manufacturers though, using different recipes, and the candy that captured the hearts of Americans was not the chewy candy kisses of Scottish fame but the Tootsie Roll.

So popular were Tootsie Rolls in the States at one time, the candy was even included in field rations for American troops during WW II.

Kerr's was founded — and still operates — in St. Thomas, Ontario.

Kerr's candy, ready to fly off the shelves.

And yes, the near indestructability of a Tootsie had much to do with the military's selection. Perhaps it is no coincidence that Kerr's would introduce its molasses candy during the same war.

Now in its 80th year of production the Kerr's candy kiss, with its distinctive orange, yellow and black wrapper, seems to defy all rules of marketing, logic or even pleasure.

Perhaps we shouldn't be surprised. It's only been 80 years. We've been wondering about winter a lot longer.

Readers' Remarks

Personally, I've always loved candy kisses and look forward to them every Halloween. Laura Secord used to make a nice, hard molasses (dark) chocolate that my mother would buy a 1/2 pound of, for me, every Christmas, now sadly unavailable. But I am in a distinct minority on this, although I've never understood why. — *Dwight*

I have always loved and still love this (unfortunately) only once-a-year candy. And I'm 62 years old! Thankfully, I have no dentures to worry about. If you happen to be given candy kisses and have no plans on using them for ingenious and industrious ways to fix stuff, fire them off to me. I'll be sure to give them a good home as they wait upon their eventual demise. — *Paul*

I love them too but did not know the history. Interesting for sure, and so Canadian. — *Larry*

I LOVE THESE and oddly enough my kids love these too! I think that this has got to be one heck of a marketing gimmick. Last year I ran into this woman that loves them so much that she was going to every store in town on November 1st and trying to buy up every bag she could. — *Faith*

I would not eat them even when I was a kid. If I could not trade with another kid for something else I put them in the garbage. I think they were the ultimate in "cheap" candy so people would buy them just to have something to put in kids treat bags. — *Peggy*

I remember the orange, white, and black (liquorice) candy kisses in the early 60s, which to me were much better. I believe they may have been from Loblaws. Sadly, I haven't seen them for decades. — *Heather*

You other commentators are crazy! Sure, I would eat them if there were no other options in the world (or in the pillow case) but they are at the bottom of the Halloween candy hierarchy. — *Alan*

Ninety-nine per-cent of my Halloween loot comprised of these kisses. I couldn't eat them fast enough. By morning of November first they would be almost gone. Started trick or treating in 1950. And I happen to love Thrills gum! — *Kathy*

Bought three 800-gram, 100-count bags. One for the children, and two for me. Not enough though. I love, love, love them! — *Linda*

Readers' Remarks

They are the best kisses ever! I have loved them since I was a child, and I am now 72-years young. I look for them every year. — *Louise*

I used to love Thrills but could never stomach these molasses candies. Even my mother, who liked molasses, didn't like them. They were always the dregs of Halloween candy — you couldn't trade them, couldn't give them away and they eventually went in the garbage. — *Rick*

I just wanted to mention that perhaps part of the demand for kisses comes from French Canadians. Québecois kids who went to Catholic school celebrated Saint Catherine's day by making molasses taffy called "tire" in French, and "pull" in English. The tradition was started by Marguerite Bourgeois the first teacher to arrive in New France. She made these candies to entice kids to come to school. Food for thought and maybe worth looking into! — *Steven*

Ok...as a kid, I hated them...I used to give then to trick-or-treaters that came after I got home and had my candy checked. Fast forward...kids of my own...they don't like them. I was going to give them away...but had one...and now am so in love with them! Maybe all I needed was a dash of maturity. — *Dirty Jeep Girl*

I'm going to go out and try to get a bag of candy kisses today! Remember the white ones? Were those also made by Kerr's? I loved them as much as the molasses ones. — *Cindy*

They were my father's favourite Halloween candy. We would take them hunting and eat them all day. That is is one of my memories. Thank you for the story. — *Diane*

When I was a kid the kisses were much darker and harder, chewier than they are now. The texture is much softer and the colour far lighter than it used to be. I loved them years ago when I was young and they had the long chew to them. Now they are too soft and do not last as long. I assume some of the molasses was removed and more sugar added. — *Nikki*

My dad loved these. So he made a haul every year, when we'd go through our bags and give them all to him. He also liked Thrills. Treats were in short supply in those days, so Thrills were about the only gum we got, along with Beeman's — *Sandra*

20 WHAT'S UP WITH THAT ISLAND BEHIND PARLIAMENT HILL?

There's a small, rocky and desolate island in the middle of the Ottawa River, behind Parliament Hill, which is a haven for seagulls. It is even nicknamed "Gull Island," although on marine navigational charts it is called "Hull Island."

It's a strange little rock. More bird than rock. Although it's proximity to Parliament Hill is intriguing. Was anything ever there?

Let's Google It

Well, yes, there was. And it's had a few different names as well, including Twin Pines Island. Let's jump in the *Ottawa Rewind* Time Machine and check it out.

This 1831engraving shows the island with trees and vegetation.

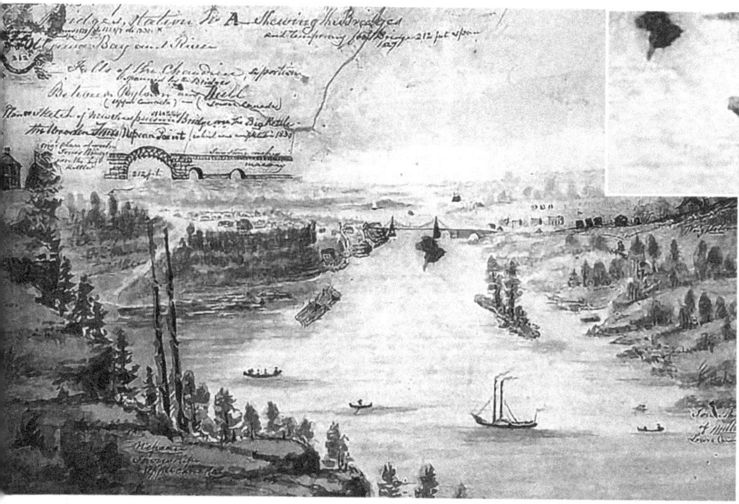

This 1832 watercolour, with steamship in foreground, shows our island the year the Rideau Canal opened.

By 1838 our island is down to two pines.

An 1840 engraving by the famous Bartlett still shows the island with two pines.

It's 1854 and our island has lost a pine. Down to just one now..

1855. Still no Parliament Buildings on top of the cliffs. And still one pine on that island.

Readers' Remarks

This is also a great place to have a campfire in the Fall, which I have done now for several years. One year, I invited Slo' Tom to sing and play guitar for us as we enjoyed the fire and ate a potluck. There are a number of wild tomato plants, a big beaver, and four bolts at the upriver end where something was mounted, perhaps a flagpole in the old days. — *John*

Thanks for the research into this island. I have another island perhaps you can look into. On Google maps it is identified as Lumpy Denommee's Island. It is located near Lemieux Island and Merrill Island in the middle of the river. I know those islands were used for logging channels, so could this be named after some crazy logger? — *Richard*

From an 1895 map of Ottawa. Is that a house?

It's 1955 and the Chaudière Falls have been dammed. There are no trees left on our island.

So there you have it — the pictorial history of that little island behind Parliament Hill. In 189 years it has gone from a forested island of pines, to two pines, to a lone pine, to no pines.

Maybe a developer will one day take it to the next logical step and put a condo building on the little island. A trendy new place that might be called Hull or High Water.

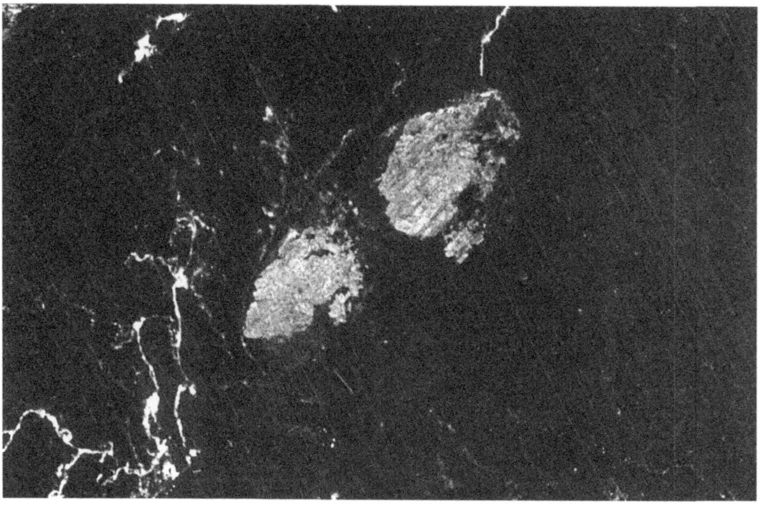

An aerial view of our island today. No house. No Pine. A lot of gulls.

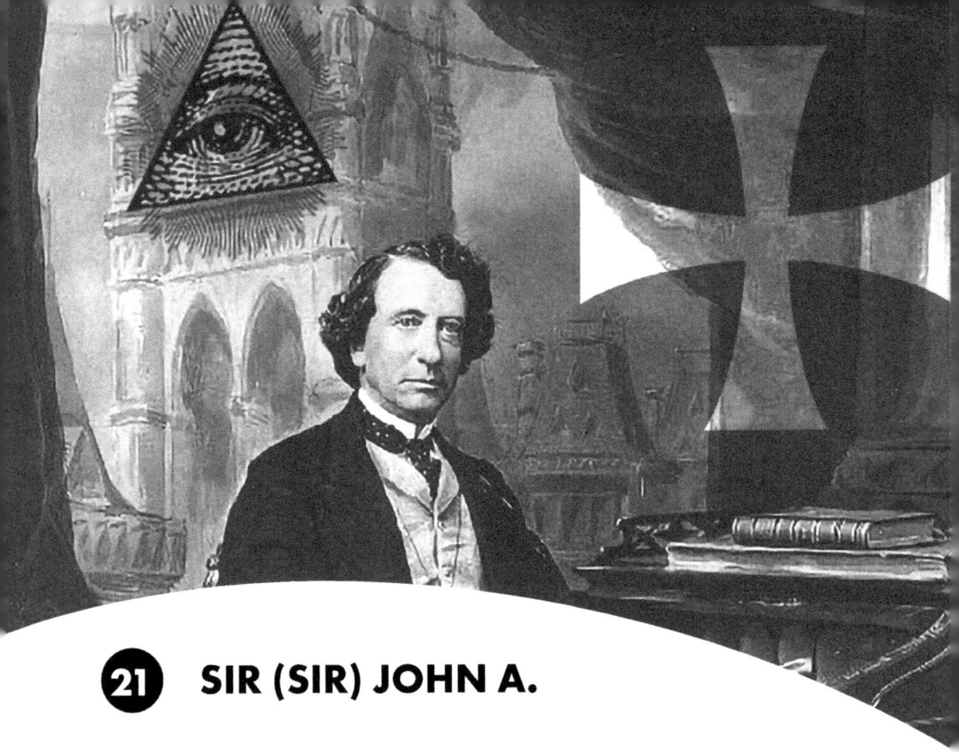

21 SIR (SIR) JOHN A.

John A. Macdonald became *Sir* John A Macdonald on the morning of July 1, 1867. Knighthood was Macdonald's reward from Queen Victoria for helping persuade four British colonies to come together and form a country.

But that wasn't Macdonald's first ascension to an order of knights. A document in the Ottawa archives shows he was appointed a member of the Knights Templar thirteen years earlier.

Sir John's First Knighthood

Macdonald's family immigrated to Kingston, Ontario in 1820 from Scotland, and it was in Kingston that John Alexander would begin his practice as a lawyer. Twenty years before the Macdonalds emigrated to Kingston, according to the 1890 document *History Of Knights Templar In Canada*, by J. Ross Robertson, the first Encampment of Templars in Upper Canada opened in that city.

The Encampment was known as "No.1 or St. John's in the Town of Kingston," and it met in the house of Sir George Millward. Macdonald would enter politics at a municipal level, serving as alderman in Kingston from 1843–46.

He took an increasingly active part in Conservative politics and by 1844 (at age 29) was elected to represent Kingston in the Legislative Assembly of the Province Of Canada. A year later he was made a Royal Arch Mason and ten years later a member of the Knights Templar.

How do we know this is true? Library and Archives Canada has a document that looks to be Sir John A. Macdonald's registration certificate with the Masonic Knights Templar. It is dated June 15th 1854 and reads:

"This is to certify that Companion John Alexander Macdonald of the Royal Arch Chapter 491 meeting in Kingston in Canada West and called The Ancient Frontenac Chapter and who was installed on the 10th day of April AL 5858 a Knight Companion of the Order of Masonic Knights Templar in the Hugh de Payens Encampment meeting in Kingston..."

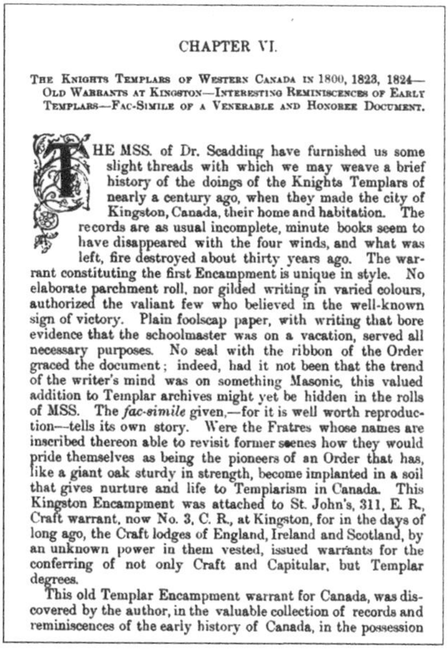

CHAPTER VI.

THE KNIGHTS TEMPLARS OF WESTERN CANADA IN 1800, 1823, 1824—OLD WARRANTS AT KINGSTON—INTERESTING REMINISCENCES OF EARLY TEMPLARS—FAC-SIMILE OF A VENERABLE AND HONOREE DOCUMENT.

THE MSS. of Dr. Scadding have furnished us some slight threads with which we may weave a brief history of the doings of the Knights Templars of nearly a century ago, when they made the city of Kingston, Canada, their home and habitation. The records are as usual incomplete, minute books seem to have disappeared with the four winds, and what was left, fire destroyed about thirty years ago. The warrant constituting the first Encampment is unique in style. No elaborate parchment roll, nor gilded writing in varied colours, authorized the valiant few who believed in the well-known sign of victory. Plain foolscap paper, with writing that bore evidence that the schoolmaster was on a vacation, served all necessary purposes. No seal with the ribbon of the Order graced the document; indeed, had it not been that the trend of the writer's mind was on something Masonic, this valued addition to Templar archives might yet be hidden in the rolls of MSS. The *fac-simile* given,—for it is well worth reproduction—tells its own story. Were the Fratres whose names are inscribed thereon able to revisit former scenes how they would pride themselves as being the pioneers of an Order that has, like a giant oak sturdy in strength, become implanted in a soil that gives nurture and life to Templarism in Canada. This Kingston Encampment was attached to St. John's, 311, E. R., Craft warrant, now No. 3, C. R., at Kingston, for in the days of long ago, the Craft lodges of England, Ireland and Scotland, by an unknown power in them vested, issued warrants for the conferring of not only Craft and Capitular, but Templar degrees.

This old Templar Encampment warrant for Canada, was discovered by the author, in the valuable collection of records and reminiscences of the early history of Canada, in the possession

From *History of Knights Templar in Canada.*

A Windowless Building, a Glass Case

What did it mean to the young country, having a Templar Knight as its prime minister? It is not difficult to imagine the Templars having a vast network of influential and powerful members within the former British colony.

In the United States Templars and Masons were involved in everything from drafting theAmerican constitution to designing the currency. Benjamin Franklin, George Washington and James Monroe were all members of the ancient societies.

Canada was just the same. Eleven of Canada's thirty-seven Fathers of Confederation are known Free Masons. They were: Hewitt Bernard, Sir Alexander Campbell, Sir Frederick Bowker Terrington Carter, Edward Barron Chandler, Alexander Tilloch Galt, John Hamilton Gray, Thomas Haviland, William Alexander Henry, William Henry Pope, Sir Leonard Tilley and Sir John A Macdonald.

Eleven of Canada's Fathers of Confederation were Free Masons.

Canada's third prime minister, Sir John Abbott, was also a member of the ancient orders.

There is one last place where you can find evidence of Canada's first prime minister belonging to this ancient and secretive society. Not surprisingly, it can be found in Kingston.

Inside the windowless lodge of the Kingston Masonic Temple, carefully preserved and protected inside a glass case, lies Macdonald's gilded apron and gauntlets, along with his regalia as Past Grand Senior Warden.

It is not known how many current MPs are Masons or Templars but I'm sure some are still there, as they have been all along. The Knights Of The Political Round Table.

↑ The Kingston Masonic Temple.
→ In the museum of the Kingston Masonic Temple, the first prime minister's gilded Freemason apron and gauntlets.

THE CHATEAU LAURIER AND THE *TITANIC* 22

Sitting atop a wooden pedestal in the Chateau Laurier is a stone carving of Sir Wilfrid Laurier, prime minister when the hotel was completed in 1911, and also its namesake. The hotel itself was the brainchild of Charles M. Hays, who founded the Grand Trunk Pacific Railway, Canada's second transcontinental rail-line. Part of Hays' vision for that transcontinental line was a luxury hotel in the nation's capital.

Built at a cost of two million dollars, the grand opening of the hotel was planned for April 26th 1912, with Hays and Laurier in attendance. Hays went on a shopping trip to London, England, before the opening, to purchase furniture for the hotel dining room. While there he met J. Bruce Ismay, chairman of the White Star Steamship Line.

Ismay invited Hays to travel home to Canada aboard White Star's newest ship; one that he claimed was the most luxurious and fastest on the high seas. Ismay said he could make arrangements to have the hotel furniture shipped on the vessel as well. Hays accepted this generous offer and paid only a small fee for his deluxe suite aboard the *Titanic*.

The Manifest That Survived

The cargo manifest for the *Titanic* is now in the US National Archives. The only reason the document still exists is because another ship carried the *Titanic* manifest.

Looking at the manifest I believe the furniture bound for the Chateau Laurier was the line entry for "3 case furniture" listed as belonging to William Baumgarten & Co. This was a London-based interior design company that worked mostly with hotels (it out-fitted the Plaza Hotel in New York City, for example.)

We may never know for certain if this was Hay's furniture, but no other shipment of furniture on the *Titanic* manifest is for more than one case. And none seem to be listed to another interior design company.

The furniture, as we all know, never made it to Ottawa. At 11:40 pm on April 14, 1912, the *Titanic* hit an iceberg and sank. Hays helped the women in his party into one of the ship's 20 lifeboats while he, his son-in-law and his secretary remained aboard.

→ Charles M. Hays, the visionary behind the Chateau Laurier Hotel.
↓ The lobby of the Chateau Laurier, with the bust of Sir Wilfrid.

The Chateau Laurier as it looked on the day it opened, June 12, 1912.

Paul Chevré, sculptor and *Titanic* survivor.

Hays, according to news reports written after the tragedy, was confident the ship would not sink and that he would join his wife later. His body was recovered floating in the Atlantic, days after the ship went down.

New furniture was ordered for the Chateau Laurier and the official opening was delayed until June 12th, 1912. With the prime minister in attendance, a subdued crowd tried to celebrate the completion of Hays' magnificent hotel.

One More *Titanic* Connection

Let's return to that carved bust of Sir Wilfrid Laurier. For this is one more Ottawa connection to the ill-fated *Titanic*.

The bust was carved by French sculptor Paul Chevré. It was commissioned by Hays. Chevré sent the bust ahead to Ottawa on another ship, but decided to travel with Hays aboard the *Titanic* for the official opening of the hotel. He got on the ship in Cherbourg, France as a first-class passenger (ticket number PC 17594, Cabin A-9) and reportedly played cards throughout the trip with other French passengers.

Chevré survived the sinking of the *Titanic*. The sculptor reportedly pocketed his playing cards, boarded one of the first lifeboats to be lowered, and escaped the fate that befell his patron and the other passengers that stayed aboard.

But Chevré never recovered from the trauma of that night and died within two years. Friends in France say he was stricken with shame when he returned home, for being one of the few men to survive the tragedy.

That's a lot of connections for one hotel to have to the most famous nautical tragedy in history. And maybe it shows in more ways than furniture and carved busts.

According to guests and staff of the Chateau Laurier, the ghost of Charles M. Hays haunts his glorious hotel. There have been reports of furniture being rearranged and objects being thrown out, as though Hays was unhappy his chosen furniture never made it to Ottawa.

True or not, the capital's connection to the *Titanic* disaster is a close one, and it may never rest quietly.

The Chateau Laurier dining room as it looked in 1912 with furniture to replace that lost on *Titanic*.

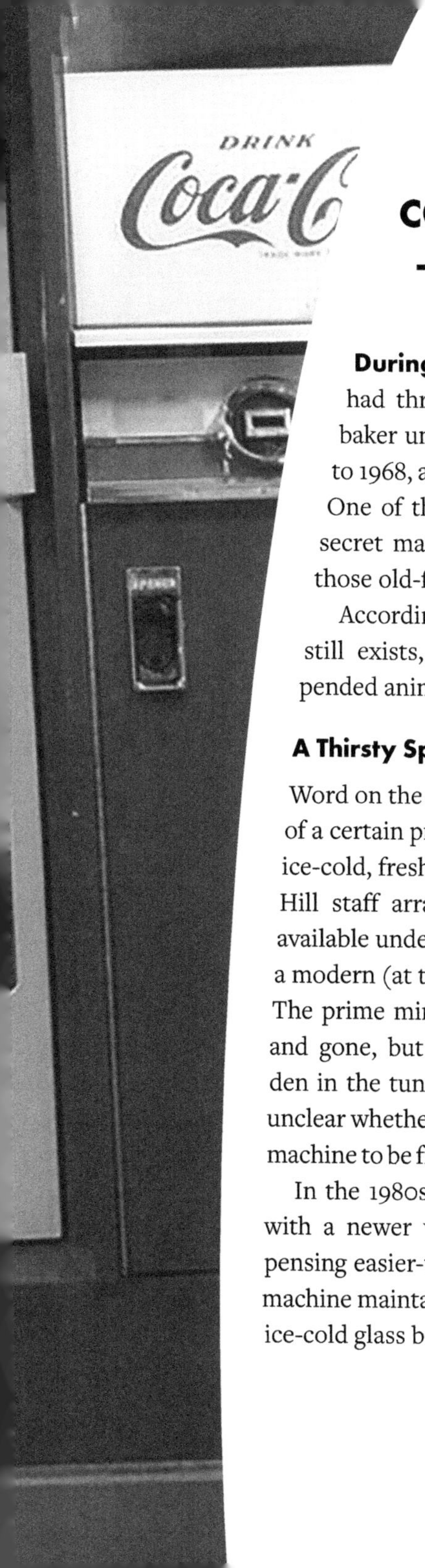

23 CAN'T FIND COKE IN A BOTTLE? — BECOME AN MP

During the Swinging Sixties, Canada had three prime ministers: John Diefenbaker until 1963, Lester Pearson from 1963 to 1968, and Pierre Trudeau starting in 1968. One of them is responsible for installing a secret machine that still dispenses Coke in those old-fashioned glass bottles.

According to my informant, the machine still exists, caught in a weird state of suspended animation.

A Thirsty Spouse

Word on the street is that in the 1960s, the wife of a certain prime minister would often demand ice-cold, freshly bottled Coca-Cola. In response, Hill staff arranged to have the freshest Coke available underneath Centre Block, dispensed by a modern (at the time) vending machine.

The prime ministers and their wives have come and gone, but the Coke machine remains, hidden in the tunnels beneath Parliament Hill. It is unclear whether a contract with Coke requires the machine to be filled in perpetuity, so I investigated.

In the 1980s, the 1960s machine was replaced with a newer version. However, instead of dispensing easier-to-handle aluminum cans, the '80s machine maintained the tradition of spewing forth ice-cold glass bottles of Coke.

A Mysterious Contract

The glass bottle vending machine that once sat beneath Centre Block.

A photograph my informant supplied reveals a pile of empty bottles beside the machine and, on closer examination, the name "Navan Vending" as the company that maintains the machine. I tried to contact the owner of the company for further intel about this curiosity hidden beneath our country's seat of power. However, Navan Vending is currently listed for sale, so I'm not sure whether the business will dissolve, along with any contract for the hidden Coke machine along, or whether a new company will be required to fulfill the contract. I haven't received a reply yet.

The Concealed Coke Machine's fate may be further sealed because the Centre Block is now closed for *10 years* for major restoration work. The Coke machine may thus be mothballed or, worse, permanently removed.

For now, all we know is that a covert Coke machine has been dispensing ice-cold bottles of refreshing cola for over 50 years beneath Parliament Hill, quenching the thirst of prime ministers and staff. I'm surprised our current prime minister did not have it replaced with a healthier organic cold-pressed juice machine, but perhaps the wood-grained relic remains for nostalgic — or contractual — reasons.

And thus it serves as a reminder that even in today's world of fake news and political lies, those who operate in Parliament still sometimes need the Real Thing, and Coke is it!

A FOLK HERO AND A SUNKEN FORT 24

In 1660, a vicious battle took place on the Ottawa River — a battle so epic that history and folklore intertwined to create an enduring legend. The Battle of Long Sault occurred halfway between Ottawa and Montreal, on the shores of the Ottawa River, and gave rise to a Quebec folk hero by the name of Adam Dollard des Ormeaux.

The exact location of this battle, however, has never been determined. Recent research has uncovered compelling evidence of a quietly shelved archeological dig in the 1950s that indicate the famous battle took place in present-day Ontario — not Quebec.

Becoming Legend

The Battle of Long Sault has become deeply engrained in Quebec's cultural history. Finely crafted into a heroic figure, Dollard embodies idyllic French-Canadian nationalism and staunch Catholicism.

The May 24 weekend — Victoria Day in the rest of Canada — is unofficially known as Fête de Dollard in Quebec. In 2003, provincial legislation officially declared the date to be National Patriots' Day. A central figure of this Quebec patriotism is a young man named Adam Dollard des Ormeaux, a 25-year-old commander of the garrison in Ville-Marie (later renamed Montreal).

In April 1660, Dollard requested permission from Governor Paul Chomedey de Maisonneuve to take an expedition up the Ottawa River toward present-day Ottawa to attack a war party of Iroquois. Dollard believed that Iroquois warriors encamped along the Ottawa River were preparing to destroy French settlements at Ville-Marie, Quebec City and Trois-Rivières.

A memorial stature to Adam Dollard and the Battle Of Long Sault in Montreal..

Dollard said he could surprise and ambush the Iroquois warriors before they could begin their campaign against New France. After assembling a force of 16 volunteer riflemen and four Algonquin warriors, including Chief Mituvemeg, the expedition left Montreal in late April 1660 with several canoes filled with food, ammunition and weapons.

Fighting the strong current of the Ottawa River, Dollard and his men finally reached their destination in early May: an area thought

The Long Sault Rapids on the Ottawa River, pre-flooding.

to be a good place to ambush the Iroquois coming downriver. At the riverside site he chose, there was already an abandoned Algonquin fort made of trees planted in a circle, cut down to trunks. Forty Hurons, under Chief Etienne Annahotaha, came to this position to assist Dollard with his ambush plans. To create a strong fortress from which to launch his attack, Dollard and his men began building a new wooden palisade around the wall of existing tree trunks, but the Iroquois arrived before his new fortress could be completed.

Héroïque défense de Dollard et de ses compagnons

Early-20th-century depiction of the Battle of Long Sault.

The Battle of Long Sault

When the Iroquois approaching from the west along the Ottawa River arrived at Dollard's position, he engaged them with musket fire. The Iroquois responded with an immediate assault made on the fort, which Frenchmen inside repulsed. The retreating Iroquois took the canoes the French had left on the beach, broke them up and set them on fire, using the burning wreckage to set ablaze Dollard's new wooden stronghold. The French and their Huron allies were able to resist the attack and, in doing so, killed a chief of the Seneca.

In a horrific and brutal scene, the French placed the Seneca chief's head on a sharpened pole of the palisade as a grim warning to the remaining Iroquois. However, the infuriated Iroquois responded by bringing 500 more warriors to the scene. The Hurons, witnessing the huge army of Iroquois, defected to the other side—except for the Huron chief, who remained loyal to Dollard.

The Iroquois built wooden shields called "mantelets" that could repel French musket balls. After a week of back-and-forth harassment, the final battle began. Now armed with their shields, knives and axes, the Iroquois chopped through the fort's walls and started pouring into Dollard's wooden stronghold.

Sensing imminent defeat, Dollard ignited a keg of gunpowder inside the fort and prepared to hurl it down on the Iroquois attackers. However, when the bomb left his hands, it struck the palisade wall, bounced back and exploded in his own fort. The Iroquois forces killed Dollard and the defenders in a gruesome skirmish that left only four Frenchmen alive — three of them quickly burned alive within the fort, and a fourth later tortured and killed. Fearing more intense battles ahead, the Iroquois retreated west. They decided not to unleash havoc in Ville-Marie, where the French likely had more muskets and cannons.

Dollard was defeated and the Iroquois achieved their revenge, but the history books say that the young Frenchman managed to scare off the attacking Iroquois, saving Ville-Marie and the rest of New France from imminent bloodshed.

Indigenous survivors of the epic battle on the Ottawa River recounted the tale in Ville-Marie (Montreal). The courageous tale of Dollard des Ormeaux and his men was then recounted to Catholic

Dedicating a memorial to Dollard in 1919 in Carillon, despite any proof the battle took place there.

nuns. They decided Dollard should be known as a heroic martyr for New France and the Church.

In the 1800s, the Catholic Church began popularizing its version of Quebec's history with an emphasis on Christian heroes, including Dollard. So it comes as no surprise that, in 1919, a small town in Quebec called Carillon was chosen as the spot for a massive memorial to Dollard. The location was picked at random, because it fit a certain narrative and was thought to be in the general vicinity of the historic battleground. No evidence was ever found of the battle taking place at that location, but it was as symbolic a place as any to celebrate Dollard's heroism, so the memorial was built.

But — the Battle Wasn't in Quebec

After developing an interest in learning where this historic fort might be located, I came across a 1960 journal article, "The Lost Battleground of Long Sault" by National Museum of Canada archeologist Thomas E. Lee, who weirdly published his report through the University of Rome. The paper clearly outlines an extensive archeological dig Lee carried out in the 1950s that uncovered a burnt-out palisaded fort — on the Ontario side of the Ottawa River. However, all this new historical evidence was soon conveniently submerged underwater, when the nearby Carillon Dam was built in 1959. It raised the Ottawa River water levels by over 62 feet (19 metres) and flooded out the rapids of Long Sault, including all evidence of Lee's archeological find in Ontario.

Using Lee's notes and the historical accounts of the battle, I sketched what I thought a 17th-century wooden palisaded fort might have looked like, then overlaid that sketch on the possible site. It seems to be about 50 feet off the shoreline of private property. If that property owner is willing, it might be worth seeing whether metal detectors could unearth any evidence of the battle, such as musket balls, arrowheads, knife blades and any other remaining 17th-century artifacts. To my knowledge, no further archeological excavations have been conducted, and the site and its secrets remain submerged.

Readers' Remarks

I would be very interested in participating in an official, sanctioned marine archeological survey of this site, before it is disturbed by "treasure hunters." I believe this site should be off-limits to the general public, at least until a proper survey can be done, so that it is not vacuumed for souvenirs. — *Mike*

There's a great deal of history and interesting stories that can be told of life on the Ottawa River over the last 300 years or so. I'm surprised that there isn't more literature out there, or maybe there is, but it's just ignored or forgotten. Your short articles are wonderful to get people thinking more about the people and events that shaped our region. — *Michael*

A great read, thanks. Those excavation photos are compelling. Interesting how this site is buried by water and political factors. — *Ian*

I paddled from Ottawa to Montreal a few years ago, locking down at Carillon. I wish I had known about this submerged fort then. If I do the trip again, I will make a point of paddling over the area to see what I can see (probably nothing). My nautical charts show Greece's Point and Chute-à-Blondeau, so I could easily pinpoint the spot. The whole river route is drenched in history. You can feel it as you pass. Thanks for posting this. — *Elano*

Thomas Lee and his archeological dig, undertaken before the building of the St. Lawrence Seaway. Images from the 1960 Journal article "The Lost Battleground of the Long Sault" by Thomas E. Lee.

THE AVRO AND THE IROQUOIS 25

At the dawning of the Cold War the Canadian government contracted Avro Canada to develop an all-weather interceptor to face what was being called "The Soviet Threat."

The government contract called for development of a two-seat, dual-engine, all-weather jet fighter. The Royal Canadian Air Force specifications called for advanced avionics and radar for what were expected to be all-weather and night sorties with Russian fighters. Avro started the project October 1946.

It asked another Canadian company, Orenda, to build the plane's engine. Orenda completed the prototype in less than a year, with the first test conducted February 1949. The CF-100's maiden flight was one year later.

When it entered production the Orenda jet engine was the most powerful in the world, and it would stay that way until 1952. Development of the engine was so top-secret — it would also be used in the Canadair F-86 Sabre fighter jet — even the test-site was classified.

In 1953 Avro again contracted Orenda, this time to produce an engine for the equally secretive CF-105 Arrow. Orenda again did a quick turn-around and delivered a prototype in December 1954.

The Iroquois engine, as Orenda called this prototype, has been the subject of speculation and fascination for decades. Test results at the time show the Iroquois engine was the most powerful in the world. It was designed for peak performance at an altitude of 50,000 feet and

Avro Arrow with Avro Canuck in the background.

The Canadian designed Avro CF-100 Canuck.

Mach 2 speed. (It was tested at altitudes as high as 70,000 feet, and forward speeds as high as Mach 2.3.)

But on February 20 1959, after 7,000 hours of testing, the Iroquois engine was cancelled, along with the entire Avro Arrow program.

The Avro's Sad Tale

The Avro Arrow has become a Canadian fable of sorts. Was the world's most advanced plane killed off by a misguided political decision made by the government of John Diefenbaker? It is a question debated in Canada to this day.

(Not only the plane and the engine were lost with the cancelling of the Arrow contract. Many of the engineers and scientists suddenly out of work found employment in the United States. A decade later, working for NASA, those same people would help land a space ship on the moon.)

↑ An Orenda engine, on display at Carleton University.

← An Avro Arrow test model, attached to Nike rocket.

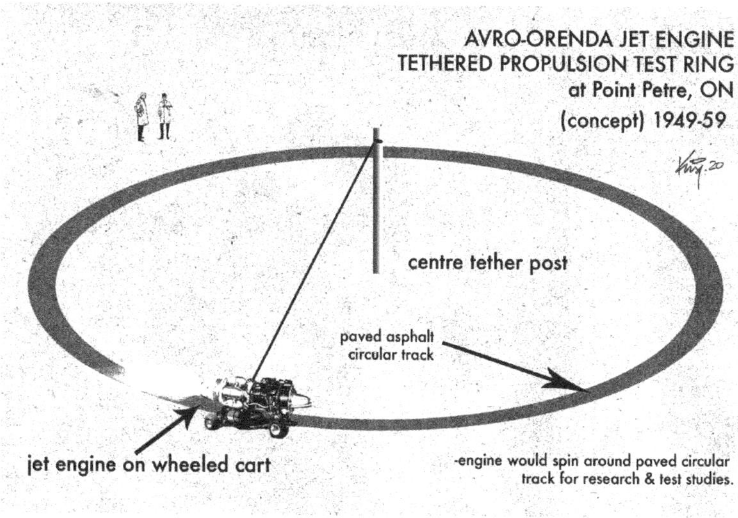

Concept sketch showing how the Orenda Ring may have worked..

Diefenbaker seemed to sense history might be less than kind to him for this decision and he was ruthless when cancelling the Avro program, ordering prototypes destroyed and files sealed.

As a result of Diefenbaker's actions (and not surprisingly) the myth of the Avro Arrow has grown mightier through the years. Anything to do with the Avro Arrow is of interest, as is the Iroquois engine.

So where did these top-secret tests occur, the ones that showed Canada had once again developed the world's most powerful jet engine?

According to *Camp Picton: A Storied 70 Years in a Canadian Military Training Camp,* written by Joanne Courneya-Fralick, the tests were conducted in a field 20-minutes south of Picton, Ontario. The location happens to be a fifteen-minute drive from my parent's home.

Looking for the Iroquois Test Site

According to Courneya-Fralick, one day in 1951-52 a military convoy stopped near a Picton school to offload jet fuel. On the bed of one truck was a CF-100 jet. After leaving the area the convoy headed toward Point Petre.

The author visited Point Petre and found an asphalt ring in a field with a large post in the middle. One way of testing a jet engine, at low speeds, early in its development, is to bolt it to a wheeled cart that is attached to a central post. When the engine is ignited it spins around

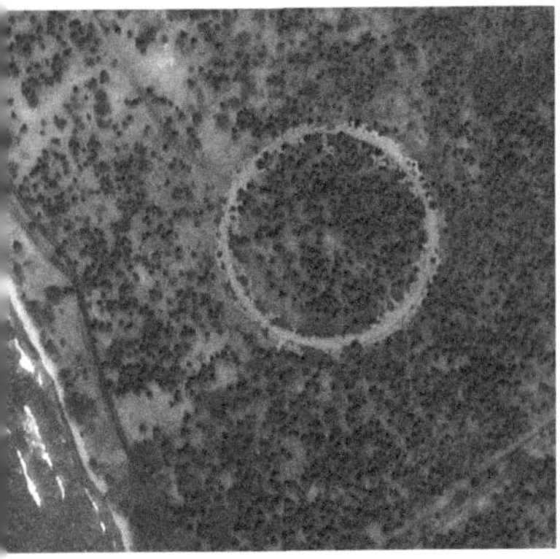

↑ An unusual ring shape in a field near Point Petre.
↗ Avro Arrow model launch pad at Point Petre as it appears today.
→ Aerial photo of Point Petre, showing the Orenda Ring.

the asphalt track, tethered to the centre post.

The ring and post that Courneya-Fralick found are less than a kilometre from a known test facility for the Avro Arrow. (It was from Point Petre that scale models of the Arrow were fastened to Nike Rockets and fired over Lake Ontario.)

So is this the top-secret testing location for Avro's fabled Iroquois jet engine? When I examine Point Petre on Google Satellite Maps I see an unusual anomaly in a field.

It is circular in shape. And it's large.

Yes, I had to go see it. The photos you're looking at on these pages show what I found.

This may indeed be the top-secret Orenda test-site. Abandoned for 60 years after the Avro Arrow program was cancelled, the test track and tether ring stand in mute testimony to what might have been.

Readers' Remarks

I was at Point Petre in November but had no idea that this was once the test site for the Avro Arrow. I only went to Point Petre because my parents took me camping at Salmon Point, starting in the early-'70s and I took my kids there until the campground closed. We could see the lighthouse at Point Petre from the campground and I always wondered what it would be like to see it up close. — *Ward*

My wife and I went camping at Sandbanks two years ago. Part of our reason for going was I have a telescope that I like to do a bit of astrophotography with. I noticed how much darker the skies are around Point Petre. Couldn't help but notice the ring on Google Earth, which really piqued my interest. — *Blair*

I went there about eight years ago, while looking the place where the Nike missiles were launched, and wound up at the place where the huge rhombic antennas were still strung up. I think the two sites must be in close proximity. — *Mike*

When in doubt — walk. Here is what I found at the Orenda Ring.

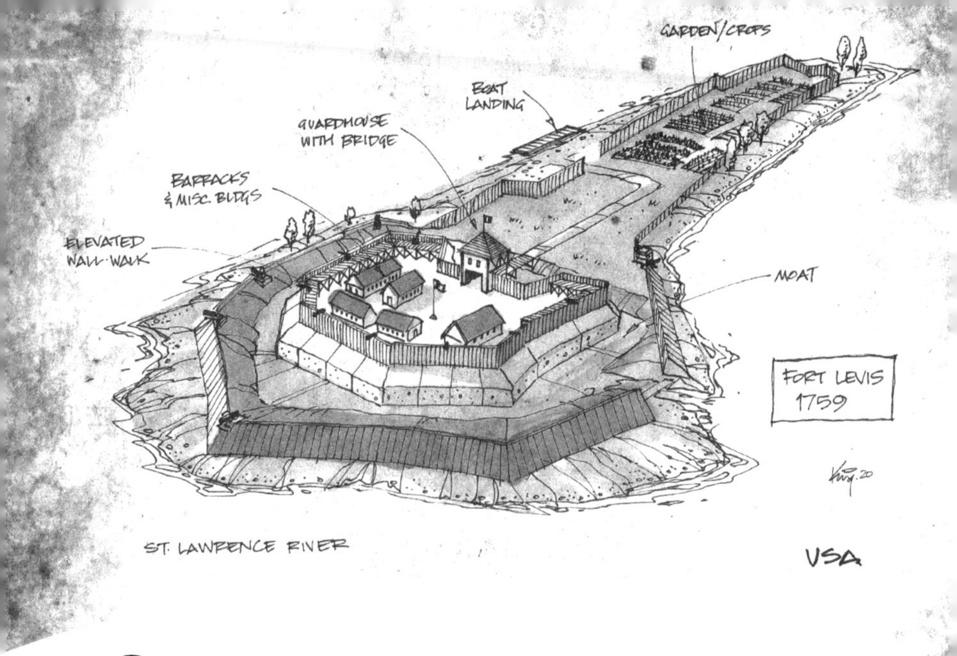

26 THE LAST STAND OF NEW FRANCE

While doing research one day on another topic I came across an excerpt from an 1876 book about forts. I thought I was familiar with the old forts along the St. Lawrence and Great Lakes — Fort Henry in Kingston being the largest and best preserved — but the book mentioned one I had not heard about before.

It was called Fort Levis. It was a French fort. It was near Prescott.

My curiosity may have ended there — another fort, I'll have to remember that — but upon further research I found out little-known Fort Levis had an important role to play in Canadian history. And important is probably a weak word. Fort Levis was where New France made its last stand in North America.

When the fort fell in the summer of 1760, the Seven Years War between Britain and France was effectively over. It would be the final battle. New France would cease to exist two weeks later, when the Marquis de Vaudreuil surrendered the city of Montreal.

Although it fell in 1760, Fort Levis would survive another two hundred years, before disappearing during construction of the St. Lawrence Seaway. Today, only a small portion of the island where the fort once stood is above water.

Could remnants of Fort Levis still be there?

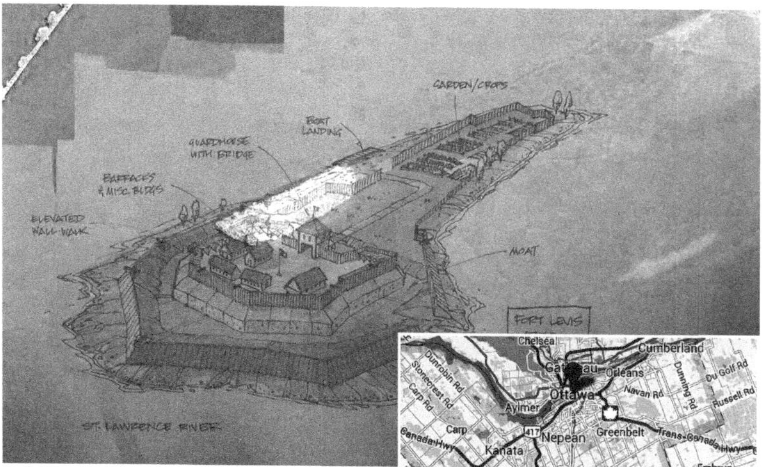

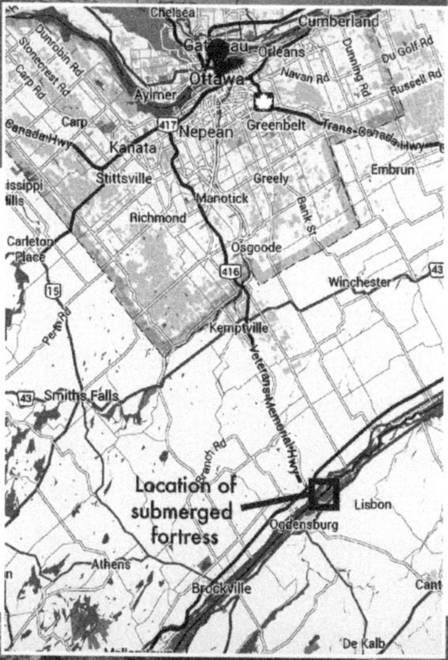

↖ A concept sketch of how the fort would have looked on Isle Royale in 1759..
↑ Whatever remains of the 1759 island fort is now underwater.
→ Map shows location of sunken fort.
↘ Isle Royale is now Chimney Island.

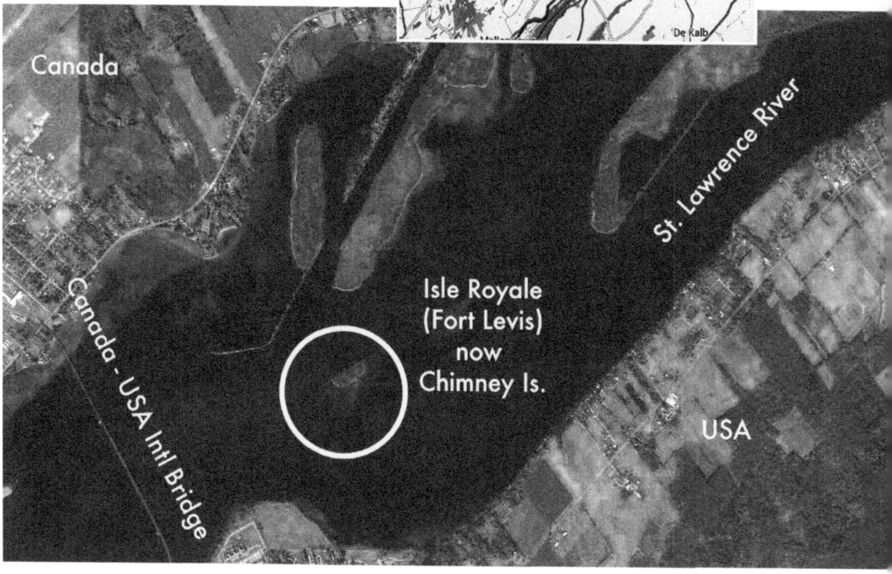

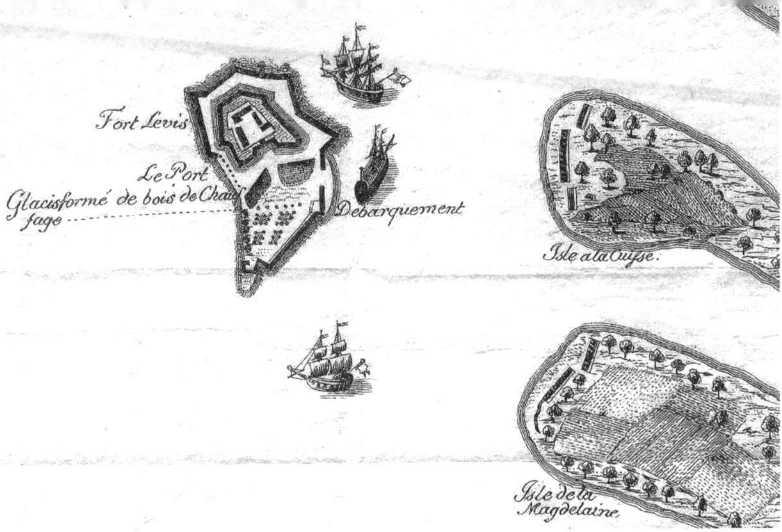

A French map from 1759 shows Isle Royale with Fort Levis.

The Last Days of New France

The French called the island where Fort Levis was built Isle Royale. A rather grand name for such a small island, but the French had big plans for the island and maybe that explains the name.

Isle Royal was where New France would build a fort intended to stop the British from advancing down the St. Lawrence River toward Montreal. The Seven Years War was going badly for New France, and it was no secret that the British plan was to surround Montreal by sending ships up the St. Lawrence River (Quebec City had already fallen) and downriver from Kingston.

New France's dire situation called for bold action, and an existing fort was abandoned (near Ogdensburg, New York) in favour of building a new one at Isle Royale. The island was better located to repel a British attack.

Originally to be built of stone, the French were left with no time for such a structure and Fort Levis was made from wood, with bastions in each of the corners. A small port was already on the north shore facing the Canadian side of the river, and this was used to bring over goods and munitions. French Commander Pierre Pouchot was given command of the fort.

Pouchot never received the big cannons he had been promised by France nor the influx of new troops, so he used the cannons and munitions stripped from the recently abandoned fort and the troops on hand. It is estimated Fort Levis had no more than 300 soldiers when the British arrived.

On the other side, as scouts had already told Pouchot, the British had a force of 10,000. Most would be arriving on two fully armed and provisioned gunships. The ships had already left Kingston.

The French troops hunkered down, stared up river, and waited for the Battle of the Thousand Islands to begin.

The Canadian Alamo

The French troops caught an early break in the battle. Perhaps their only one. The British gunships *Mohawk* and *Onondaga* got lost in the maze of the Thousands Islands for a week before finding Fort Levis. This gave the French more time to prepare for the coming battle, which finally commenced on the morning of August 19, 1760.

The British were under command of Major-General Jeffrey Amherst, who had captured a French gunboat during his lost week in the Thousand Islands. Amherst had renamed the ship the *Williamson* and so it was three gunships that surrounded Fort Levis that August morning.

In addition to the ships British troops had also taken up positions on nearby islands, placed cannons there, and these big guns were part of the battle.

Despite the ships, the artillery positions and the vastly superior fighting-force numbers, the first day did not go well for the British. The newly captured *Williamson* was hit 48 times by cannon fire and had to retreat. Amherst called a ceasefire shortly afterwards.

British gunships *Mohawk* and *Onondaga* advance up the St. Lawrence.

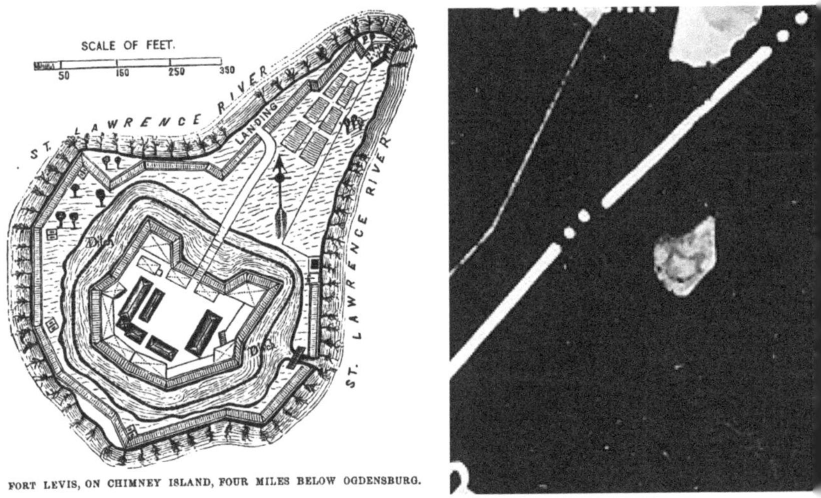

A British map from 1760 shows the captured French fort. It was renamed Fort William Augustus.

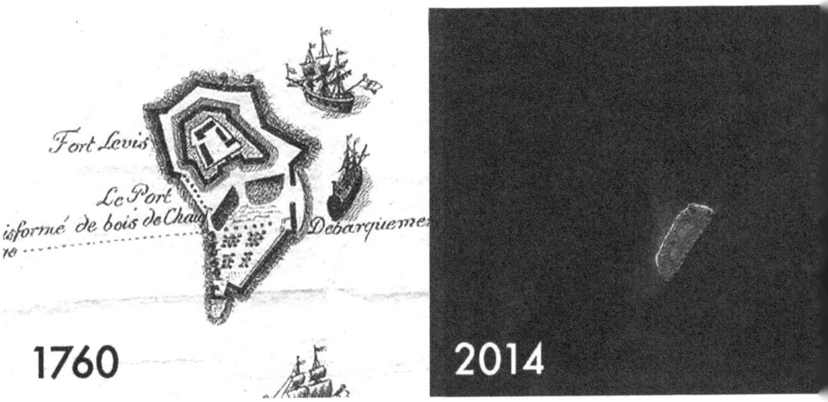

A comparison of the island in 1760, and today, after building the St. Lawrence Seaway..

At dawn the British resumed the attack. Again the *Williamson* came under an intense barrage of cannon fire and this time the French sank the ship. Not long afterwards, the French cannons also sank the *Onondaga*. And not long after that, French troops repelled a British ground assault on the island.

Amherst, convinced that the superior size of the British force would ensure victory no matter what setbacks he encountered that day, pressed the attack.

Then the French sank the *Mohawk*. Amherst called another ceasefire.

The British commander was surprised by the tenacity of the French troops. With British victory in the Seven Years War all but ensured, Amherst had wondered whether there would be any resistance at all from Fort Levis. The French cause was lost.

But as three sunken ships told him rather convincingly, the French had a different take on the situation. So that night Amherst ordered his cannons to switch to "hot balls." This was cannon fire meant to set ablaze whatever it struck.

On the third day of the Battle of the Thousand Islands Fort Levis was soon afire. Having no more cannonballs or gunpowder — and soon to have no fort — Pouchot finally surrendered. Amherst renamed the fort Fort William Augustus and continued on his way to Montreal, where he would join British troops already surrounding the city.

It is estimated the French lost 275 men during the Battle of the Thousand Islands. The British lost 26. It was a valiant and courageous defence of Fort Levis by the French, and at best, it delayed the final surrender in Montreal by a week.

No wonder some historians refer to the Battle of the Thousand Islands as Canada's Battle of the Alamo.

It is unclear what happened to Fort Levis between 1760 and 1950, when the St. Lawrence Seaway began construction. A study of aerial

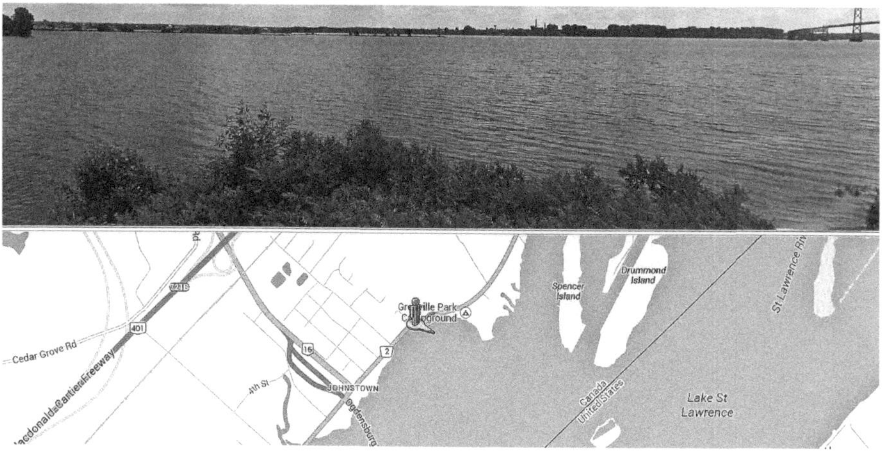

A view of Chimney Island from the Prescott International Bridge.

images produced in 1954 show that the ruins of the fort were still visible then. Whatever remained, though, was buried or slipped under the water when the Seaway was completed in 1959.

All that remains today of this important and decisive piece of Canadian history is a small patch of rock and grass that is now called Chimney Island. It can be seen, just slightly to the east, when you travel over the Prescott International Bridge.

Readers Remarks

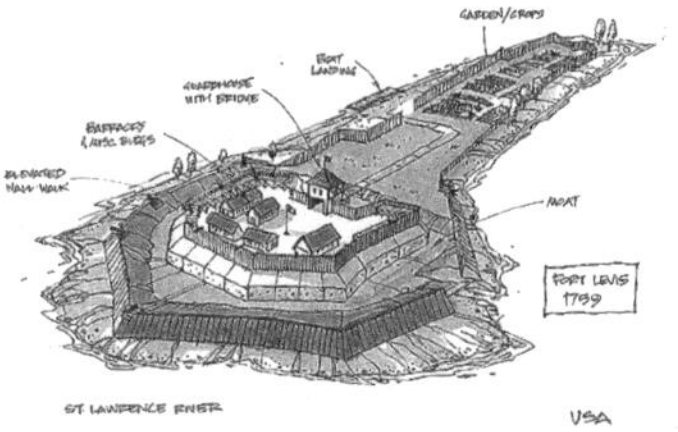

I believe the greater part of the island was destroyed by the construction of the Seaway; not merely flooded but excavated into oblivion. — *Michael*

Ruins of the fort — well preserved for several hundred years due to the fact that no farming/tilling was ever done on the island — were extant prior to construction of the Seaway. It likely was among the best-preserved period forts on the continent, but it was destroyed. A horrible shame. I have in my possession musket balls as well as a British coin from the early part of the 18th century which I found on the island many years ago. — *Ted*

To make room for the shipping channel, the north half of the island was removed and dumped onto the south half of the island. More likely the remains are still on the remaining portion of the island. However they would be under several feet, or more, of dredging debris. — *Olde River Man*

I grew up in Prescott during the building of the seaway and had never heard of this historic event. Thanks for sharing. — *Tom*

It was reported that there was a chapel on the island. Before the French surrendered they took anything of value, put it into the barrel of one of the cannons, and dropped it into the river to prevent the English from capturing it. This tale was related to me by several of Fort Wellington's curators over the years. How true it is, who knows? Interesting story. — *Charles*

I was born in Prescott, and I know of this Fort. I left Prescott in 1957, just after the seaway started, and there was a lot of talk about it back then. — *Ronald*

I couldn't tell you how many times I've crossed that river (where Fort Levis was.) Wow. ... More news, more history. Thanks — *Larry*

This is a fascinating story and a real tragedy that this historic fort was destroyed during Seaway construction. Sometimes we are so short sighted. — *Ben*

27 HARTWELL'S SILVER LINING

Here's an odd fact about the Rideau Canal you may not know. During its construction between 1826-32, and although canal labourers were employed by the British military — many were paid in American half-dollars.

The reason for this is because their wages came from an indemnity the United States paid to Great Britain after the War of 1812. The indemnity came in the form of silver half-dollars.

The wages for the canal labourers were packaged in kegs and sent upriver from Montreal. The kegs were later distributed to paymasters along the canal route. Paymasters were in Ottawa, Kingston, Jones Falls, Smiths Falls, and Hartwells, the lock-station at the southern end of Dow's Lake near Carleton University.

A keg of American silver half-dollars in work camps filled with itinerate labourers was a security concern to the British military (perhaps you can imagine that.) To see just how *serious* a concern it was, take a tour of the Bytown Museum.

The museum is located in the building where the Ottawa paymaster's office would have been. The "safe" where the keg of coins was stored is still there for visitors to see. And it would have been quite a feat, getting in and out of that safe without getting caught.

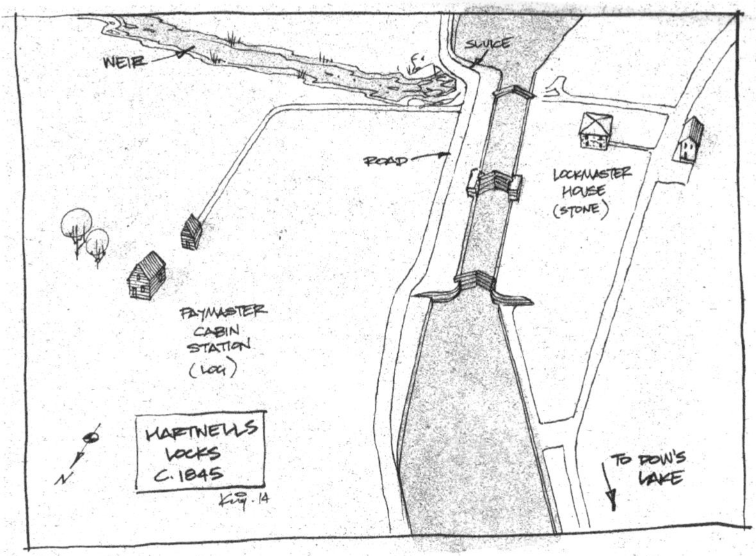

↑ A sketch of Hartwells Locks as it may have appeared in 1845.
→ An 1830 American silver half-dollar.

Story of the Second Lock

That a paymaster's office would be at Hartwells (the very first lockstation after Ottawa) may seem surprising. But it shows — may even be the best example out there — of how difficult it was to build the northern end of the Rideau Canal.

It was brutal work. And after building the six locks that connect the Ottawa River to the Rideau River (the largest on the system); after blasting through more rock than they would blast for the next fifty miles; after finding a way through Dow's Great Swamp (a place so inhospitable John Burrows went back to Ottawa the first time he tried to survey it) — after all that, reaching Hartwells must have seemed like entering another country.

(Today, it is not a ten-minute drive.)

So Hartwells had its own paymaster's office. Along with other things you don't see at most lockstations (although each one is different and charming in its own way.)

The lockmaster's house at Hartwells, for example, is also a concealed fortress. The original building was stone and designed to withstand an attack. There are three "blockhouses" along the Rideau

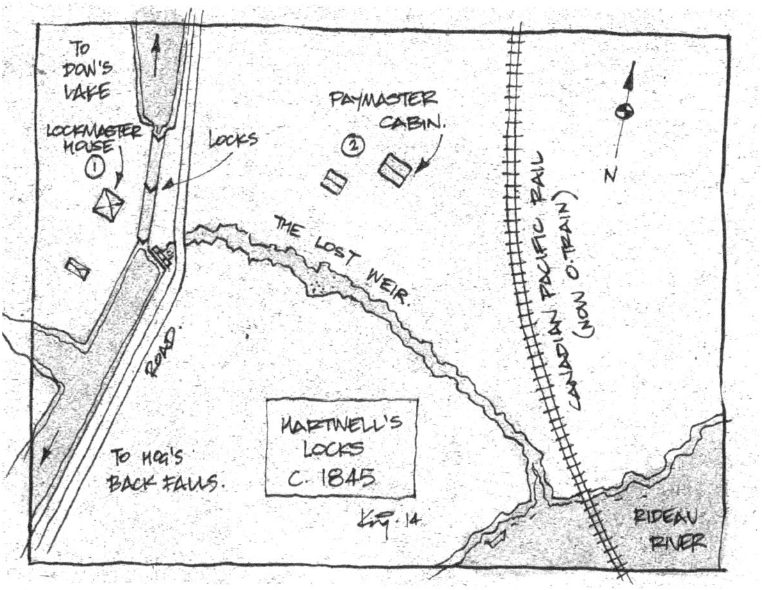

A sketch of the area in 1845. Note the bywash weir.

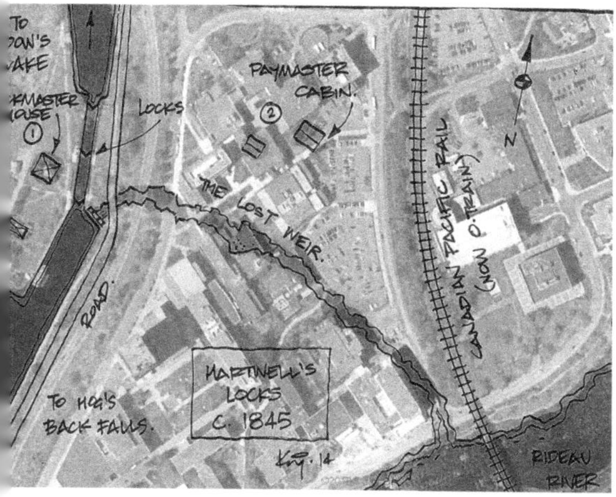

↑ Original stone Lockmaster's House now covered in clapboard. ← "Ghost" map shows the original 1845 map and a current aerial map.

Canal that *were* small forts (they can be found at Merrickville Locks, Narrows Lock (Big Rideau Lake) and Kingston Locks.) The stone building at Hartwells was a step below a blockhouse, and it was later covered in clapboard siding, which is how you see it today.

Hartwells was also built with a bywash, to carry overflow water from the Rideau River across what is now Carleton University. Originally built as a weir, the channel was an open creek that cut across the land to the east of the locks and emptied into the nearby river.

Readers' Remarks

My grandfather was Allan Moses. He was quite a character. Unfortunately he passed away in 1961, a few years after his retirement from the Rideau Canal. And he never found any buried treasure. Thanks for the great article. I'm very proud of my family's history with the Canal. My mother was born in the Lockmater's House at Hartwells. — *Deborah*

A sluice gate was used at the side of the locks to monitor the weir waters, and the gate is still visible. The weir was operating, as John By designed it, until the late-'50s when it was diverted with culverts as part of building Carleton University

The Legend of Hartwells Missing Treasure

Hartwells has one other thing many lock-stations don't have. A cool missing treasure story.

In 1953 the lockmaster at Hartwells, when asked what his plans were after retirement, said he planned on finding the missing keg of silver coins. Allan Moses then told of a theft that happened at the lock-station long ago, with the thief having to bury his stolen loot to evade capture. The thief planned on returning later but never did.

Legend or Retirement Plan

Whether Moses was repeating a legend that came with the lockstation, or whether he had found evidence to support the story is unclear. But he claimed that "a great deal of money was stolen from the paymasters house (during construction of the Rideau Canal.) It was in an old log cabin across the canal from the lockmasters house."

No one knows if Moses ever found the silver coins, or if his story was true. But it's a fun tale to wonder about (one silver American half-dollar from the1820s could be worth as much as $600 today.)

Using a sketch from 1845 and a Bing Maps aerial image of the area, I was able to draw how Hartwells may have looked in 1845. You can see where the paymaster cabin is, and what is there now. It seems Carleton's engineering building was constructed over the spot.

Was the lockmaster's story true? Is there a keg of silver coins buried beneath the campus of Carleton University, waiting to be found? Given the strange history of Hartwells Locks, I wouldn't rule anything out.

28 A MISSING OTTAWA SIGN

There was a time when visitors flying into Ottawa were greeted by an impressive display of civic pride — the word OTTAWA spelled out in giant letters next to the airport.

How big was it? The six words would have measured 500 feet in length, and 100 feet in height. The letters were probably white stone or chalk and likely were part of the Ottawa Flying Club's original runway, which opened in 1928.

The letters would have also marked the site of CFB Uplands, part of the Royal Canadian Air Force wartime training station of the British Commonwealth Air Training Plan. It opened in 1942.

There was a time when Ottawa, with both CFB Uplands and a private airport terminal on the same site, had the busiest airport in Canada. It reached its peak in 1959, with 307,079 aircraft take-offs and landings.

So whatever happened to that giant Ottawa sign? Using geoOttawa and current aerial maps I was able to trace the fading of the letters over time, watching them almost disappear. They are faint, but still visible today.

↓ Pilots training at CFB Uplands during World War II.

→ The Ottawa sign in the grass of the air field.

The 500-foot Ottawa sign, as seen at CFB Uplands in 1965. Below, the sign as seen through the decades.

Readers' Remarks

I always look forward to your discoveries. On Google Earth, if you follow the Timeline back to 10 April 2007, there is a really sharp photo of the sign. — *Doug*

I so enjoyed this story! Thank you. — *Elizabeth*

Just spent 25 minutes looking at it on Google Maps. Fantastic find. — *John*

Circa 1991.

Circa 2002.

Circa 2007.

Circa 2016.

IN SEARCH OF THE FIRST HOUSE 29

The history of Canada's national capital region is filled with stories of endurance and perseverance, of overcoming great obstacles in a land of dense forest and jaw-dropping swamps. The Algonquin had no permanent structures in the area and it was not until the first settlers arrived that buildings appeared.

But where *was* the first house in the national capital region? To my surprise, I soon learned that we don't know.

In some cities, that wouldn't come as a surprise. When you start going back millennia, the record keeping becomes sloppy. And where would a city like Rome even begin? Their founding story is a myth.

But the national capital region *has* a founding story. It has a founding settler. Both the story and the settler are well known. It all happened just a little more than two centuries ago.

So where is the darn house?

The Story of Philemon Wright

The first settler to the national capital region was an American named Philemon Wright. He came in 1800. (Not sure if this case is unique but most Canadian cities have British or French founders, with the prairies having some Eastern European founders.)

↑ Philemon and Abigail Wright.

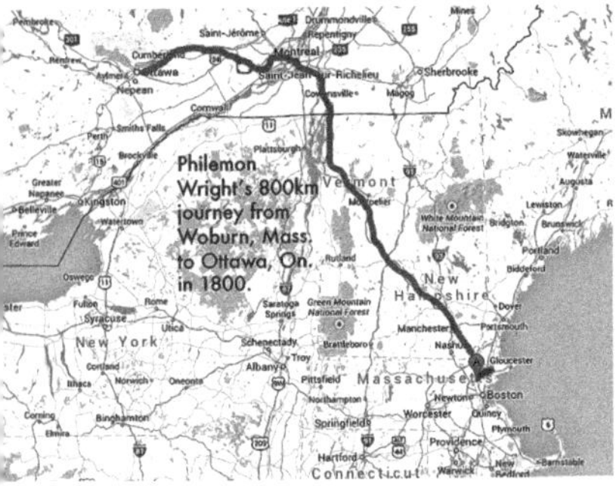

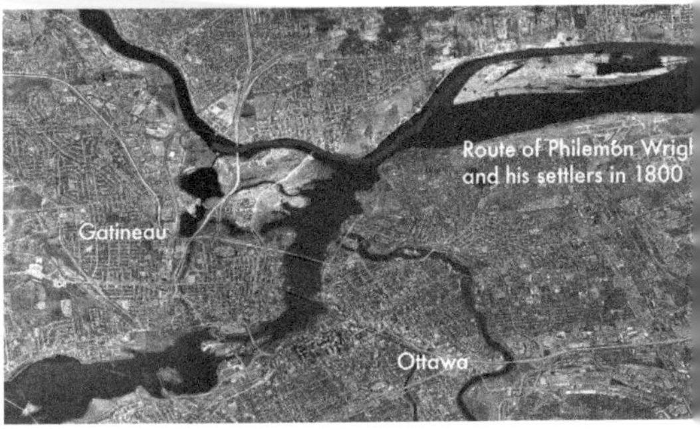

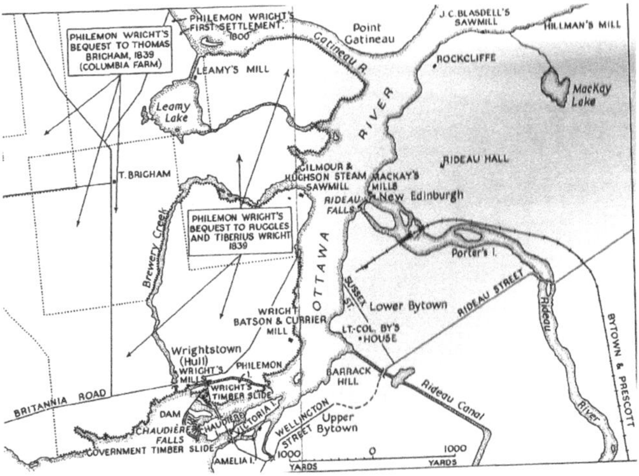

↖ Wright's 1800 journey northward from Massachusetts to Ottawa.
↑ The journey from Montreal to Ottawa.
← A map showing both Wright's and Leamy's properties.

Wright was from Woburn, Massachusetts and he dreamed of having his own country estate one day, a dream that had little chance of success around Boston, where land was already becoming scarce and costly. Wright was a methodical man though, and he began searching for places in North America where land was still plentiful and cheap.

The Ottawa-Gatineau area fit his requirements rather nicely. The British government was offering generous land grants to encourage settlement inland from the St. Lawrence River. And the grants didn't get much more generous than they did around here.

The British had yet to survey the Ottawa River past Chaudiere Falls. So when Wright looked at a map of what land

As Wright's first cabin would have looked.

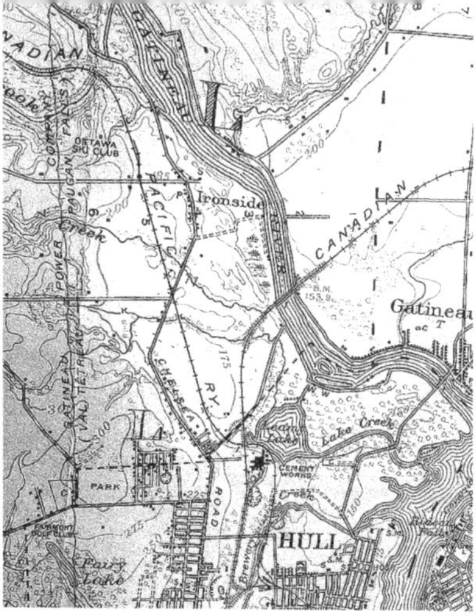

1935 Department of Defence map showing building at the end of the Wright farm road.

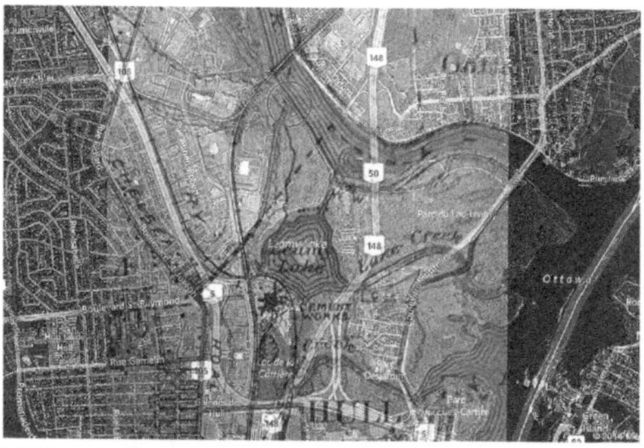

1935 map ghosted over current aerial map.

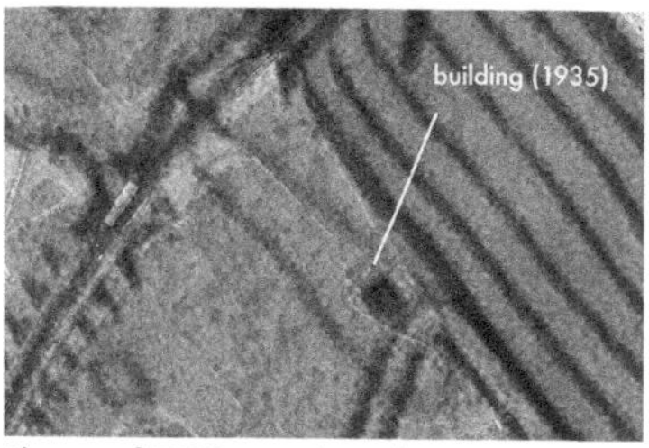

Closeup of 1935 map ghosted over current map.

Using GPS coordinates, the location of Wright's first settlement was established

The location of House One.

was available, the Ottawa region would have been at the edge of the map. (Imagine the map as stadium seating. Now imagine Ottawa-Gatineau as the last row.)

After visiting the area Wright was impressed and he applied for a land grant with the British government. He first had to swear an oath of allegiance to His Majesty, the King of the British Empire, and then his application was approved.

Wright convinced a number of his Woburn neighbours and family to come with him and he set out from Montreal in February 1899 with a party of 50 men, women and children. The settlers travelled down the St. Lawrence River and then up the frozen Ottawa River, aided by

A mass of tumbled stones on the site could be remnants from the first settlement.

Walking down the Capital's first road.

an Algonquin hunter who met the settlers not far from Montreal and must have felt sorry for them. He escorted them all the way to the Chaudiere Falls.

Wright's land grant was on the north shore of the Ottawa River, and his first cabin was built in what is now Lac Leamy Park. The river embankments were twenty-feet high and the settlers climbed atop, started clearing land and building cabins.

Wright soon had his home, tilled fields and a road leading to the Chaudiere Falls, where he would soon open his first mill. As Wright started to prosper he moved from his log cabin to a home in Wrightsville, the town that had sprung up around the Chaudiere Falls and that would later become the city of Hull. In 1835 Wright sold his original cabin and lands to Andrew Leamy.

Clues, Clues, So Many Clues

One of the frustrating things about trying to locate *House One*, as I already mentioned, is that you would expect the task to be easy. The house isn't *that* old. Nobody disputes it. Yet we still don't know where it is. (Ambiguity. Maybe it's an Ottawa thing.)

Here's the story: we know where the house must have been built. It is NCC land, within Lac Leamy Park, in the city of Gatineau.

Readers Remarks

This is a fascinating report, thank you for all your efforts. I always wondered about the old farm. I agree the NCC should mark the site and indicate clearly where the first house stood. Maybe politics comes into play. Who knows? — *Larry*

Such a fascinating and ultimately sad story. If nothing else, a commemorative plaque belongs on or near the location researched in this article. I can hardly believe something this historically significant has been lost/overlooked. — *Diane*

Excellent historical research and it certainly indicates that we have not been doing a very job in this region in terms of marking and recognizing our historic sites. At a minimum, we need more historical markers and plaques. Thanks for doing undertaking this work — *Donald*

Thank you for taking such a keen interest in Philemon Wright. I am one of Wright's many descendants (on my mother's side, he was my great grandmother's great grandfather). — Jonathan

Bravo for all these research efforts, which are intended to pay homage to our past. To understand where we come is to better choose where we are going. — *Bervil*

A log building that was still standing in an 1884 photo of Leamy's farm is probably *House One*. How can we say that? Because Wright — it really *is* clue after clue — left a detailed description of the cabin in his memoirs:

"*... built of undressed tamarac logs in true rustic shanty fashion. The chinks between the logs and scoops of the roof were caulked with mass, driven in with a thin pointed handspike, over which a rude plaster of blue clay was daubed. The chimney was very wide and low, and was built above a huge boulder which formed the back of the fireplace. There was no upper story to the rude dwelling, which was partitioned off into bedrooms at each end, with a large living room, kitchen, dining room all in one, in the centre.*"

And then there's this. You can't even call it a clue. The NCC claims to have *found* the house.

The text below comes from an NCC website:

"*While stabilizing the shoreline of the river, the NCC conducted archaeological salvage excavations at the site of Wright's original house. A wealth of domestic items were found, including earthenware pots and dishes, cutlery, buttons, religious medallions, combs and dolls.*"

And later:

"*It was the conclusion of another archeological dig at that site that the foundations of that house dated from the early 19th century. The location was reburied for preservation and protection and the NCC has plans for future commemoration of the site."*

The archeological investigation referenced by the NCC was conducted in 2006. But we still haven't been told where the site is. Or seen any of the artefacts the NCC claims it took from House One

When in Doubt — Walk

What other choice did I have? I needed to take my maps and find the house myself. Packing a camera and GPS, and joined by fellow history buff and friend Glen Gower, we headed off to Lac Leamy Park.

We easily located the original road connecting Wright's cabin to his mill at Chaudiere Falls. This would be the oldest road in the region, but it is abandoned and you would never guess at its historical importance.

Nearby we found many stones spread over an area of about ten-square-feet. The stones could easily be the remains of a chimney, or fireplace. We discovered a deep pit near the stones, that could have been an outhouse latrine, or a well.

The area where we found the stones and pit are just as described in Wright's memoirs — 20 feet from the shoreline of the Gatineau River, atop a steep embankment.

Is this spot — a barren, unsightly tract of land off an NCC bike path — the site of our *House One*? I think it is.

Which still leaves me with questions. There are many plaques honouring Philemon Wright, as well as namesake schools and streets. But why no marker for what is effectively ground zero for Canada's national capital region?

Some mysteries, even when you think you've solved them, remain a puzzle.

In 1980 a plaque to Philemon Wright was unveiled in his hometown of Woburn, Mass.

TALE OF THE GUARDIAN 30

On November 4, 1989 one of the most bizarre and unexplained UFO sightings of all time occurred just west of Ottawa. It is the tale of an extraterrestrial craft that supposedly crashed in a swamp west of Ottawa near Manion Corners. Today, for UFO seekers and believers around the world, it is known simply as the "Guardian Case."

A Strange Letter

The story began when Tom Theofanous of the Canadian UFO Research Network (CUFORN) received a package from someone calling himself the "Guardian." There was no return address on the package. Inside was a hand-written letter claiming an alien craft had been recovered from a swamp in West Carleton, and that both Canadian and American military personnel had assisted in the salvage.

Graham Lightfoot, a UFO researcher living in Ottawa at the time, was dispatched to Manion Corners to interview local residents about the Guardian's claims. Some people he interviewed were mentioned by the Guardian in the letter.

Diane Labanek, a resident of the area, said that on the night of November 4, 1989, she witnessed a bright light pass overhead, heading towards a swamp south of her home. She said she also saw several helicopters earlier that evening using lights to scan the area.

Another resident said their cattle were scared by something in the sky that night and it took most of the next day to recover them. Another told Lightfoot of a very bright light that shone through their south-facing bathroom window that night. "It reached right down our hallway," the woman said. She also recalled hearing helicopters that evening.

So — some anecdotal evidence but far from definitive proof of an alien crash landing. Without verifiable proof of a crashed UFO and no photographic evidence of any kind, the case was deemed a hoax and the Guardian a crackpot.

However, if we read that note today, thirty-one years later, and if we use modern research techniques to check out the claims made by the Guardian — well, it gets more interesting.

Below is an edited transcript of the original letter sent to Tom Theofanous:

"Canadian and American Security Agencies are engaged in a conspiracy of silence, to withhold from the world the alien vessel seized in the swamps of Corkery Road, Carp, in 1989.

UFO sightings in the Ontario region had intensified in the 1980s, specifically, around nuclear power generating stations. On Nov. 4, 1989 at 20:00 hours, Canadian Defense Department radars picked up a globe shaped object traveling at phenomenal speed over Carp, Ontario. The UFO abruptly stopped, and dropped like a stone.

Canadian and American Security Agencies were immediately notified of the landing. Monitoring satellites traced the movements of the aliens to a triangular area (see aerial map) off Almonte and Corkery Roads.

The ship had landed in deep swamp near Corkery Road. Two AH-64 Apaches and a UH-60 Blackhawk headed for the area the following night. The helicopters carried full weapon loads. They were part of a covert American unit that specializes in the recovery of alien craft.

The area west of Ottawa that matches the *Unsolved Mysteries* clip about the Guardian.

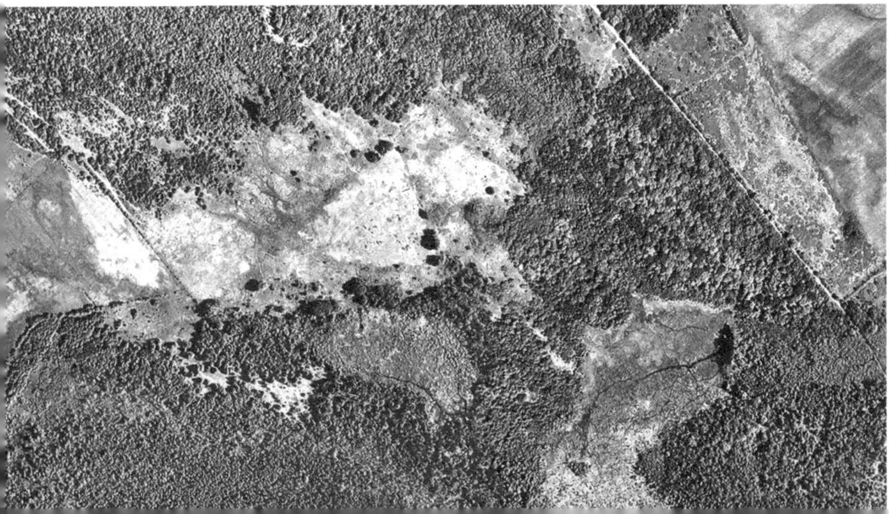

Flying low over Ontario pine trees the Apache attack choppers soon spotted a glowing, blue, 20-metre-in-diameter sphere. As targeting lasers locked-on, both gun-ships unleashed their full weapon loads of 8 missiles each. All 16 were exploded in proximity bursts 10 metres downwind from the ship.

The missiles were carrying VEXXON, a deadly neuro-active gas that kills on contact. Exposed to air the gas breaks down quickly into inert components. Immediately after having completed their mission the gun-ships turned around, and headed back across the border.

Now the Blackhawk landed, as men exploded from its open doors. In seconds the six man strike team had entered the UFO through a seven metre, hatch-less, oval portal. No resistance was encountered. At the controls, three dead crewmen were found.

With the ship captured, the US Air force, Pentagon, and Office of Naval Intelligence were notified. Through the night a special team of technicians had shut down and disassembled the sphere. Early the next morning, Nov. 6, 198,9 construction equipment and trucks were brought into the swamp. The UFO parts were transported to a secret facility in Kanata, Ontario.

As a cover story the locals were informed that a road was being built through the swamp. No smokescreen was needed for the military activity as Canadian forces regularly train in the Carp region. Officially nothing unusual was reported in the area, although someone anonymously turned in a 35mm roll of film to the National Research Council of Canada, in Ottawa. The film contained several clear shots of an entity holding a light (see photo on page 117.) At this time the photographer is still unidentified.

The humanoids were packed in ice and sent to an isolation chamber at the University of Ottawa. CIA physiologists performed the autopsies.

The reptilian, fetus-headed beings were listed as CLASS 1 NTE's. (Non Terrestrial Entities) Like others recovered in previous operations, they were muscular, grey-white skinned humanoids.

The ship was partially reassembled at the underground facility in Kanata. Unlike previous recoveries this one was pure military. Built as a "Starfighter," it is heavily armed and armoured. In design no rivets, bolts, or welds were used in fastening, yet when reconstructed there are no seams. The UFO itself is made up of a matrixed dielectric magnesium alloy. It is driven by pulsed electromagnetic fields generated by a cold fusion reactor.

The Allen Institute in Montreal where CIA-funded experiments were conducted.

All offensive capabilities utilize independently targeting electronic beam weapons. In the cargo hold were found ordnance racks containing fifty Soviet nuclear warheads. Their purpose was revealed by advanced tactical/combat computers located in the flight deck.

The most important alien-tech find were the two-millimetre spheroid, brain implants. Surgically inserted through the nasal orifice, the individual can be fully monitored and controlled. The CIA and Canadian Government have actively supported mind-slave experiments for years. Currently the University of Ottawa is involved in ELF wave mind-control programs. A continuation of the CIA psychological warfare project known as MKULTRA, started at the Allen Memorial Institute in Montreal.

Using ELF signals transmitted at the same wavelength the human brain uses, the researchers could subliminally control the test subject. The alien implants utilize the same principles except that the whole unit is sub miniaturized and contained in the brain. Fortunately the implants can be detected by magnetic resolution scanning technology. All individuals implanted by the aliens are classified as Zombies."

OK, lets stop at the zombies. This is ridiculous and an obvious piece of fiction. But — let's see if anything in the Guardian's letter checks out.

Claim One

"Monitoring satellites traced the movements of the aliens to a triangular area (see aerial map) off Almonte and Corkery Roads."

Not sure about the monitoring satellites, but the Guardian seems to know his geography. Zooming in on the "recovery area" using a

Goggle satellite map, there is indeed a triangular area of land adjacent to a swamp.

A triangular area, as Guardian mentioned, is near the "crash site.".

Claim Two

"Two AH-64 Apaches and a UH-60 Blackhawk headed for the area the following night. The helicopters carried full weapon loads. They were part of a covert American unit that specialized in the recovery of alien craft."

Once again, not sure about most of these claims, but numerous witnesses reported at the time, and have since reported, that they heard helicopters on the evenings in question.

Claim Three

"The UFO parts were transported to a secret facility in Kanata, Ontario."

In Kanata, at Shirley's Bay, there is a government research facility that oversees classified Defence Department experiments and projects. Called *Defence Research & Development Canada*, the department and its Kanata facility have long been the subject of UFO speculation.

The DND research facility near Kanata.

Claim Four

"The CIA and Canadian Government have actively supported mind-slave experiments for years. Currently the University of Ottawa is involved in ELF wave mind-control programs. A continuation of the CIA psychological warfare project known as MKULTRA, started at the Allen Memorial Institute in Montreal."

It is true that the MkUltra program operated mind control experiments from the Allen Institute in Montreal during the 1960s. Extremely low frequency, or ELF, has been the subject of many conspiracy theories over the years.

Has Anything Changed since 1989?

Well, the Guardian's claims seem more interesting today then they did back then, but it is still anecdotal evidence and far from conclusive, or at times, plausible.

As if to silence his critics, in 1991 the Guardian sent Theofanous another letter, this one claiming *another* UFO had landed near Ottawa, at the exact same spot as the alleged crash site of the first.

This package contained a video, which the Guardian claimed showed the alien craft. That video was featured on an episode of *Unsolved Mysteries*, the television show hosted by Robert Stack.

Which doesn't make it true. Just — like much of the Guardian story — slightly more interesting. We may never know what really happened around Manion Corners in November1989. Unless someone reading once worked at that secret Kanata laboratory or witnessed an alien autopsy at the University of Ottawa.

A still from the *Unsolved Mysteries* story about the Guardian.

THE MYSTERY OF THE VANIER BUNKER

31

This historical search started with a YouTube video. Many of them do nowadays.

This one was shot in Vanier by Bloeski's Wrecking Crew, which inserted a camera inside what looks like a sealed bunker in Richelieu Park. The video shows a vast room with pillars and other structures, but there is no definitive answer as to what the structure may be.

I went out to have a look. This is what I discovered.

The structure is easily accessible. It is right in Richelieu Park in an area well used by dog walkers and a walking trail runs directly in front of the "bunker." A buttressed concrete wall, about 40-60-feet long, runs along the north face of a 12–foot mound. There is an entrance portal with an eroded date — 1944 — that only became visible when I rubbed snow across the inscription.

The concrete walls are decaying and there are iron support-tie-rods visible. A small crevice is there, made by curious onlookers. The mound surrounding the entrance seems to be about 50-60-feet square and is approximately 12-feet in height. There is a cement-cross at the southeast corner of the mound.

The sealed entrance to the Vanier mystery bunker.

A date of "1944" became visible when snow was rubbed across an inscription above the sealed entrance.

There is a 12-foot-high mound surrounding the concrete wall.

So what is this?

A cement cross sits on the southeast corner of the mystery mound.

A nearby fence separates our bunker from Beechwood Cemetery, which is home to the National Military Cemetery. This cemetery was created by the Department of National Defence in 1944 for the interment of Canadian veterans. Was this odd structure a crypt or mausoleum intended for military purposes but never used and later abandoned?

Further exploration of the property, however, revealed a previous tenant for these lands. In 1938, the land in Richelieu Park was purchased by a catholic missionary order known as The White Fathers. The White Fathers were founded in 1868 and worked in Africa primarily.

The Vanier land was used to train missionaries and a number of structures were built on the property, including a sugar shack that is billed today as North America's only urban sugar shack. The surrounding maple forest is billed as North America's only urban maple syrup farm.

The White Fathers owned the Vanier property until 1976. Further research into the missionary order, and the history of Richelieu Park, reveals the purpose of our mystery bunker. According to a website once used by the City of Vanier:

"Another construction, somewhat more mysterious, is also present behind the cross, in the forest. Along the path, a shelter was dug in the solid rock and solidified with concrete and steel cables. This construction served as a root cellar for the White Fathers' crops. Like many other religious orders, the White Fathers cultivated the land and this cellar allowed them to store their harvests during the cold winter months as well as during the

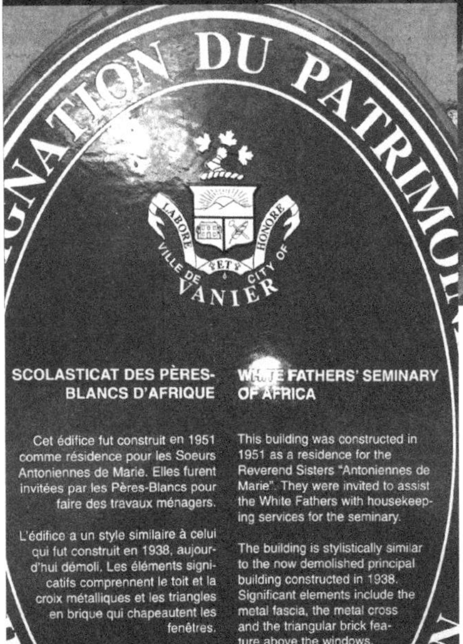
DU
LABORE
ET
HONORE
VILLE DE
CITY OF
VANIER
SCOLASTICAT DES PÈRES-BLANCS D'AFRIQUE
Cet édifice fut construit en 1951 comme résidence pour les Soeurs Antoniennes de Marie. Elles furent invitées par les Pères-Blancs pour faire des travaux ménagers.
L'édifice a un style similaire à celui qui fut construit en 1938, aujourd'hui démoli. Les éléments significatifs comprennent le toit et la croix métalliques et les triangles en brique qui chapeautent les fenêtres.
FATHERS' SEMINARY
RICA
This building was constructed in 1951 as a residence for the Reverend Sisters "Antoniennes de Marie". They were invited to assist the White Fathers with housekeeping services for the seminary.
The building is stylistically similar to the now demolished principal building constructed in 1938. Significant elements include the metal fascia, the metal cross and the triangular brick feature above the windows.

Historical gate post and statue of Our Lady of Africa, part of the former White Fathers' seminary (now Richelieu Park)

summer months. Construction of the cellar began in 1943 by digging with an excavator in the rock. The White Fathers completed the work in November of 1944 by covering the cellar with soil using a bulldozer."

So there you have it — a missionary root cellar. It is an unusual structure and an interesting piece of Ottawa history, worth a visit next time you're in Vanier.

32 REMEMBERING THE GREEN VALLEY

As a high school kid in 1990, one day I drove the Old Prescott Highway from Kingston to Ottawa in my '73 VW Beetle. I passed by a neat old diner at Baseline Road and Prince of Wales Drive on my way to an interview at Carleton University.

The Green Valley restaurant looked like part of a 1950s movie set. The white building would later burn to the ground on New Year's Eve 2002, its history disappearing in smoke and its remains bulldozed into a nondescript parking lot. For those of you who may never have known the majestic Green Valley, here's the story of this fine old dame.

W. J. Stewart
Green Is His Valley

In 1933, Waldorf Stewart moved to a remote wooded property on the Old Prescott Highway near Ottawa, and he built a play cabin for his daughter near his new home. The rustic cabin soon had uninvited guests: passing tourists who thought it was a motor court cabin rental. This type of accommodation was springing up all over North America, as more and more tourists travelled by car. Stewart realized an opportunity when he saw one. He built a few more cabins and

One of the first, if not the first motel in Ottawa was the Green Valley Tourist Court, located at the corner of Prince of Wales and Baseline Road that opened in 1933..

opened the Green Valley Tourist Court, with cabins to rent for tired travellers on their way into the Nation's Capital.

In 1947, Stewart expanded his tourism empire at what was once considered the outskirts of the city. He opened the Green Valley Restaurant, a modest diner to serve breakfast and dinner to customers staying in his 24 rental cabins. Stewart thought the motel and diner would only be open for the summer tourist season, but the restaurant gained a reputation for fine-quality food, created by a chef who had formerly worked at the Engineers Club in Montreal. After only a short period, the Green Valley became one of Ottawa's premiere dining destinations.

The Green Valley restaurant in its hey-day.

The restaurant was expanded three times and included the Then and Now Shop, where visitors could purchase toys, souvenirs and curious gadgets. Kids especially enjoyed the Mickey Mouse sundae: a scoop of ice cream with wafer ears and pistachio eyes. Many Ottawa residents will remember going there with grandparents or on special occasions.

In 1956, Stewart once again expanded the restaurant to include the Walnut Room, a special dining area with rich walnut panelling and thick carpeting. Once staffed by 65 employees, the Green Valley became an empire, but like most empires, it eventually faded away.

When I received my first paycheque from my first full-time job, I wanted to treat myself to a nice dinner. So I picked the place I saw

A menu featuring full-course meals, only between 5:30–8:30 p.m.

The cottages at the Green Valley Tourist Court.

when I first drove into Ottawa a few years earlier, the Green Valley. It was 1995 and I remember the place looked like it was trapped in 1955. It had a musty smell and was now tired and empty, staffed by elderly servers who had probably worked there when it first opened and still wore their original uniforms. The furniture was worn, the food was bland and the place felt like the setting of "The Shining." Nevertheless, you could sense it was once *the* place to eat in Ottawa. However, with the Lone Star opening up down the road and other restaurants emerging, the Green Valley was left behind, its grandeur tarnished.

I'm glad I got to visit the Green Valley before it burned down and its charred remains were bulldozed, turning this once-special place into a parking lot. Today, you would never know that site was once the location of Ottawa's grand dining experience, the now-lost Green Valley.

The former entrance to the Green Valley Restaurant, now blocked off, and turned into a parking lot.

STEWART'S GREEN VALLEY RESTAURANT, OTTAWA, CANADA.

Readers' Remarks

Thank you for this — it brings back so many wonderful memories, particularly the Mickey Mouse sundae and the gift shop in which I coveted treasures from the far east. It all seemed so exotic to this suburban Ottawa girl. — *Lostandfound Books*

Great story. I have lived in Ottawa for 11 years and had no idea this place ever existed. I have driven past its location numerous times paying no attention to the area. Thank you for connecting the past to the present and giving me and others a new perspective of our history. — *Neal*

Thanks for this–I was hoping you would do Green Valley at some point. It was an anachronistic yet beguiling place. Quite mysterious how it burned down when it did. Just what we need: another parking lot. — *Michael*

I had a few little birthday parties here. Their mickey mouse sundae has never been achieved anywhere since. The Gift Shop — top notch! That photo of the interior is exactly as it was. — *Laursica*

Many memories of special family gatherings at the Green Valley. None as special as our 1977 wedding reception. We both still miss the ambience of the Walnut room 40-gr-8 years later. — *Cameron*

Totally remember that restaurant — but had no idea that there was once a camp there. Love your blog! — *Tracy*

ABOUT THE AUTHOR

Born in Kingston, Ontario, Andrew moved to Ottawa in 1991 to study Industrial Design at Carleton University. During his time at Carleton he contributed to the *Ottawa Citizen*'s comics page with a weekly strip entitled *Off the Wall* that was carried by King Features Syndicate and published in newspapers across North America. Andrew followed his love of cartooning and was accepted into the Television Animation program at Algonquin College where he graduated with Honours in 1997. After graduating, Andrew began working in television with a number of local animation studios, as well as studios in Vancouver, Montreal and Toronto.

Andrew still resides in Ottawa where he continues to work as a visual artist (represented by Mad Dog Gallery of Picton, Ontario) and freelance designer. Andrew also contributed a regular column to the *Ottawa Citizen* that solved local historical mysteries and continues this research today in his popular website *Ottawa Rewind*.

Ottawa by foot...

As I Walked About

A Collection of Walking Columns from the Ottawa Citizen

PHIL JENKINS

OttawaPressAndPublishing.com

Read the original . . .

OTTAWA REWIND
A BOOK OF CURIOS AND MYSTERIES

ANDREW KING

OttawaPressAndPublishing.com